T0129122

LAMA
SABACHTHANI

LAMA SABACHTHANI

Is God Really Omniscient?

Emeka Anonyuo, Ph.D.

authorHOUSE®

AuthorHouse™ LLC
1663 Liberty Drive
Bloomington, IN 47403
www.authorhouse.com
Phone: 1-800-839-8640

Published by AuthorHouse 03/19/2014

ISBN: 978-1-4817-5034-9 (sc)
ISBN: 978-1-4817-5033-2 (hc)
ISBN: 978-1-4817-5032-5 (e)

Library of Congress Control Number: 2013908241

Table of Contents

Dedication

To the Way, the Truth, the Life, and the Light of the world, Yeshua Messiah, who said, "Behold, I will not leave or forsake you. I will be with you, even onto the end of times."

ACKNOWLEDGEMENTS

My unbounded gratitude to all the Prophets, scribes, dreamers, and visionaries past and present.

To all my teachers of the Holy Bible; to my parents Samuel and Suzanna Anonyuo; and to my humble, godly wife, Connie, who directed the research team, read the text at the introductory and intermediate stages, and in other ways contributed significantly to the success of this effort. Her immense contributions qualify her as a co-author, but she, as always, is satisfied to be my helpmate. I am also grateful for the priceless experiences that I gained from my children whose (Igbo/Nigerian) names encapsulate our eternal gratitude to Adonai;

Ifechi: Adonai's Light (Celebrating Yeshua Messiah); *Chidiomimi*: Yahweh is unfathomable, *Onyekachi*: Who is greater than Elohim, and *Tobechukwu*: continually praise, worship and exalt Jehovah El Shaddai. My grandchildren's names also testify to the acknowledgment of the legacy of Jesus Messiah: Amaris Chidinma, Judea, Yisrael Judah, and Ethan Olisaemeka.

I would like to pay tribute to the following servants of the Lord, who in different ways, positively touched my life: Sister Gail Johnson, Pastor Matthew Onwuka, Siamak David Shabodaghi, and Ramin Yazdani Isfehani, also, Rabbis

Humphrey Sr. and Jr. of *Rosh Pinah Synagogue*, and Dr. Joe Rosenfarb, the Rabbi of *Beth Messiah Synagogue*, all three of whom advanced my understanding of the roots of the Holy Scriptures. There is no easy way to paint my gratitude to Aiden W. Tozer, and Leonard Ravenhill, my most influential spiritual mentors, whose thoughts and teachings greatly enriched my knowledge and understanding of Adonai and the Word He spoke. The e-Bible and other web resources were of immense assistance, too.

For every author and book, Adonai forms an editor. For me, he is Dick Harrington, Ph.D (Emeritus Professor of English), a man whose passion and hunger for Truth nearly exceed my own. Thank you, Dick.

Feel the Book; in the following mail exchanges between the editor, and the author; as compiled by Connie Orumbie-Anonyuo

Emeka, I'd like you to know that, although I do wish to be paid for my services, I accept work as a writing coach/editor only if I feel personal compatibility with the author and genuine attraction to the subject and writing project . . .

I feel strong personal compatibility with you and strong personal attraction to your subject and writing project, especially given your gift of language to engage readers, guide them on a profound spiritual journey, and inspire them to achieve true spiritual transformation . . . . I respect and admire your work . . . Your manuscript fascinates me, and I feel honored to read it. I'm deeply moved by your immense faith and by your rich, powerful vocabulary for expressing your faith, knowledge, and understanding. Each page resonates with the presence of the Almighty.

Your understanding of your subject is indeed vast. As well, you embody the rare capacity to embrace and express that which surpasses understanding . . . . , you speak as a man of great experience, knowledge, wisdom, and faith . . . ~Dick

Emeka, Now I'm back—ready to work with you to produce the best possible book.

In retrospect, it was unreasonable of me, as your editor, to consider my own views regarding the suffering of Jesus on the cross. To help myself get clarity, I read about the major heresies in the history of Christianity and also consulted with a dear old friend and colleague, . . . , who left college teaching at the age of 50 to study in a seminary and is now the very fine pastor of a . . . church nearby.

What most electrifies me at this moment, besides finally attaching and sending the document, *is my having come to see the rightness of your vision as against the vision I'd held and wished to hold onto.* It seems premature to explain what I mean, but in time I'll gladly do so ~Dick

Greetings, Emeka~ ". . . You show remarkable power to engage readers in your journey of doubt, fear, struggle, revelation, triumph, and belief and to present and explain your discoveries. ~Dick . . . Just as Bible stories, such as Job's, compel and teach us, your own "story" as a student and follower of the Almighty and the Word has the potential to compel and teach readers with varying degrees of belief. ~Dick

Good morning Emeka. ". . . Please let me know your thoughts and feelings about my request for you to provide considerably more narrative and description of your pertinent outer life.~Dick

Good evening Dick. ". . . one may end up with a biography which puts me in the spotlight, instead of the message given by Adonai.

See Dick, I want this book to be what I believe very strongly that I was commissioned to do; *Tell the world that Adonai does not, has never, and will never forsake anyone who puts his/her trust in Him; and secondly, that He did not abandon Christ, as secular-humanist theologians have erroneously interpreted :Eli, Eli . . ."* ~Blessings, Emeka

Dear Emeka~I agree that your book must not become a "Romanized" autobiography of Emeka Anonyuo. My attempt yesterday to illustrate my point with my own quickly-wrought story failed because it lived too much in the material world. I regret having gotten off track . . . . The text engages me, conveys your message, enlightens me, and moves me.

I've changed my thinking about the need for more narrative and description of your external life.

I respect and appreciate your vision of the book, as well as your commitment to it, and will do my best to help you achieve your vision.
Peace, ~Dick

Emeka~ "As usual, I'm much impressed by the profound, transcendent expressiveness of your writing, and I applaud the additions to Chapter One. They contribute much to the revelation of your spiritual journey.

Emeka Anonyuo, Ph.D.

". . . I have enjoyed working on your book, and I feel confident you are saying what must be said in ways that will be compelling, thought provoking, and convincing for readers.

All best wishes,
~Dick Harrington

PREFACE

Though a labor of love, how hard it has been to transcribe and synchronize the multitude of fragments of information initially recorded in my many journals of thoughts, dreams, trances, and visions spanning thirty years. How hard it has been because of my belief that each and every fragment is an echo of God's Voice, a precious painted tile that has deserved to be discerned correctly and placed meaningfully to create a coherent, expressive whole. At the center of the mosaic is Adonai Yeshua, surrounded by tiles extending outward in a radial pattern, hopefully enabling the mosaic to achieve symmetry and meaning. How hard it has been, too, because of my awareness, as the messenger, that the book would target primarily Christian readers, many of whom, as products of human history, may hold modernist or secular humanist perspectives on the Holy Bible and especially the Personality of the Almighty. Such perspectives humanize God and elevate mankind. I believe in the Pure Divinity of Adonai and present this book to counter such God-diminishing perspectives. I am no prophet. I am simply a contemporary man who believes in the Divine with all my heart. I hear the Voice of God speaking through me. He is the book's real author.

I hope readers will appreciate the intended symmetry: the studied, steady repetitions that form patterns of ideas presented and re-presented. Consider, if you will, the concept of Emphasis and Subordination in, for example, music: when a symphony orchestra spotlights its new violin virtuoso, the other instruments play more quietly than normal so as to feature the rich, expressive tones of the solo violin. Yes, I have intentionally asserted and reasserted the key ideas of the book, so that each and every reader actually hears the alarming truth of our contemporary spiritual condition and comes to realize that what choice we make literally seals our fate for eternity. Hell? Heaven? Which will it be?

God Almighty has many names and titles, such as Jehovah, *HaShem*, *Adonai*, and *Elohim*. By describing His Personality, His Divine Attributes, and by citing evidence from the Holy Scriptures, I counter contemporary claims of God's fallibility, by demonstrating beyond doubt that Adonai does not ever equivocate and does not ever forsake us, His children. This concern, one of a group of key issues at the heart of the book, is legitimized by the findings of a survey. Professing Christians were asked this one question: Is Adonai really Omniscient, Omnipotent, and Omnipresent? Overtly and covertly, most respondents answered in the negative: No, He is not. Some respondents did answer with a simple no. But, others' hesitations and, in most cases, their stories of negative events in their lives, which they blamed on God, were harbingers of their beliefs. What is your answer?

Test How Much You Really Believe and Trust God

Consider the following clue-question. The Holy Bible, the Word of God, records that the Prophet Jonah was swallowed by a whale. Such is believable in part because our rational mind discerns that a whale can physically swallow a man. But what if the Bible said that Jonah swallowed a whale? Would you still believe the Word of God without question? In many passages of the Holy Scriptures, Adonai says that He will never leave us or forsake us. Scores of God-debunking theologians and other Bible commentators, past and present, have amassed tempting evidence to prove that Adonai is fallible, has forsaken us, and will continue to forsake us. Whose words do you believe? The words of humans, who are fallible, or the Word of God? Why do you believe what you believe? An eighty-year-old great-grandmother we met during our survey answered thus: "If God the Father said once that He will not forsake me, if my righteousness is in Christ, don't bother showing me ninety-nine other instances where He said that He would. Study the context and you will find that, as always, someone is mistaken, and it is not my God [speaking those words]." What do you think? Is she right or wrong?

If a group of the world's most trusted archeologists and anthropologists should announce, at the end of a forty-year research project, that they have found the body of Jesus Christ, would that claim rock your faith, tempting you to backslide or even fall away? Or do you have the unshakable faith that would keep you standing on the Solid Rock, Jesus the Messiah, after each storm has passed? I hope your mind is drawn to Apostle Paul's warning that believers in Christ should reject any teaching or preaching that would propagate another Christ than He whom the apostles followed—even if such new teachers were angels!

For readers who are or wish to be true Christians, key issues include the infallibility, immutability, and inerrancy of God and the Holy Scriptures. Of core significance is what the venerable Yeshua Messiah said from the cross on the day when Innocence was found guilty and crucified. What did Jesus mean in crying out, "My God, my God, why have you forsaken me?" Was His cry that of a frightened and desperate Son who had lost faith and hope in God, His Father? Or was Jesus Fulfilling a very important Divine Intention: schooling mankind in how to seek God's Aid when in despair? Alas, Christian thinkers, past and present, have failed to comprehend this crucial Divine Purpose in Christ's impassioned words. Was the Messiah a man? Was He half man, half God? Or was He God in man's body? Our answers to such questions determine the core of our spiritual beliefs.

This book draws strong parallels between ancient Greco-Roman pagan cultures and postmodernist culture, prevalent in contemporary secular-humanist churches, where teachings encourage the deification of man, the humanization of God, and subsequent equality with the Godhead. This perniciousness is energized by mankind's belief that we have become the center of "our" universe and the measure of all things. Many theologians and pastors have discarded fear of the Lord, whereas fear of the Lord is the commencement of wisdom. In their hell-inspired campaign, they teach that Adonai will suspend His Will to fulfill the desire of our hearts, because we are "the epitome of God's creation." What arrogance! With this rearrangement of hierarchy, God seems reduced to a powerless, disenfranchised spectator, who must recant His Word and endorse rebellion as self-indulgent, narcissistic mankind claims lordship of creation and sovereignty over the universe.

This "democratizing" of God and Christianity is accompanied by run-away fragmentation of the body of Christ, evident in the limitless planting and germination of colors, fragrances, and flavors of Christian denominations as well as branches of theological perspective. This pastor teaches that God's chauffeur drives a Maserati Sedan. That seminarian paints God as our buddy in a Ford pick-up. In reaction to this festering spiritual plague, the book debunks core untruths, both unbaked and half-baked, falsehoods taught by church leaders and seminarians because they fail to believe in, follow, and emulate Jesus the Messiah. Many church congregants and seminary students seek the Truth and deserve much better than contemporary spiritual culture offers.

The Book at a Glance

The mosaic design of the book allows for a multitude of headings. Each encapsulates the message of the paragraphs that immediately follow it.

The list of key topics, below, is not chronological:

Joining the choir.

What the author has tried to do.

Who is on the Lord's side? The testimonies of prophets and saints of God as to the Lord's Inerrancy and Omniscience.

Repetitious on purpose: hammering home the theme "God does not equivocate." He is Omnipresent, Omnipotent, Omniscient, Good, Just, and Worthy, and He does not forsake His Children. Above all, contrary to popular teachings, "My God, my God, why have you forsaken me?" does not translate to Adonai's abandoning His Son.

Obedience is God's Beloved Song: "If you love Me, keep My Commandments." Grappling with the audacious attacks on, and revisions of, the Holy Bible, as Pastors seek gold, silver and diamonds, the Word is compromised, and politicians flirting with the electorate in exchange for their votes, repeal the Law of God. Virtue is tarnished.

The Law: Kinship between the *Torah-Tenach*, the "Old Testament," and *Brit Chadasha*, the "New Testament." Did Jesus Christ destroy the Laws, or did He both fulfill them and strongly reestablish and reaffirm them?

In the pursuit of freedom and happiness, obey God.

As it was with Prophet Ezekiel.

Are there still true Prophets: looking at A. W. Tozer.

A majority of Christians say that God equivocates, They seem to have evidence. Can they ever be right?

Seeing Immutable God as like ourselves: fallible mankind.

The humanization of Adonai, and the deification of ourselves.

A new aphorism: why good things happen to bad people.

God did not forsake Adam, Eve, Cain, or King David. Why would He forsake His Son Jesus?

To fully understand God, we must think like Him.

If God says it, that settles it, right? No, postmodern secular humanist preachers/theologians see it differently.

When rationalists present God.

To be forsaken versus the feeling of being forsaken. In the Book of Ruth, Naomi asked to be re-named Mara because she felt that Adonai had abandoned her. Was she right? Millions in the past and present have felt the same way: forsaken by God. Are they right?

The fabrication of a "Buddy" God whom mankind can manipulate.

Does God suffer amnesia, groping and stuttering through His plans?

Preachers preach it, but is "it" the Truth that God the Father forsook His only begotten Son?

Seminary education and theological scholarship: the bastardization and undermining of the Holy Bible.

Inconsistencies and bare-faced contradictions in multiple interpretations of the Holy Bible equip the enemies of Adonai as they denigrate the Church.

A wretched portrait of God by detractors masking as angels of God's Kingdom.

Forsaking God through disobedience and rebellion: abandoning the Lord's Protective Shield.

What do people mean when they proffer that God turned His back on them? The truth, literally and metaphorically, is that Adonai has no back to turn on any one. He is Ubiquitous.

Adonai does not send anyone to hell. Individuals make that decision. "Choose you today whom you would serve." Choose one of these: the wide gate or the narrow gate.

A soothing melody that God sings: "I will never forsake you." But do we believe Him?

God perfected Job in the crucible of suffering.

The Messiah.

The visible Godhead.

Why was He born, and why did He have to die?

Yeshua was not an option. He was God's original plan.

Why did Jesus always insist that His apostles watch Him? He was and is a Model Teacher, a Life to emulate, the Way, and the Truth. Did Christ consider calling down angels to assist Him, or was He the Model Teacher teaching His disciples?

The true Messiah as against the one that mankind made.

A Paradox: Christ outnumbered and overwhelmed by His enemies?

Ridiculous: Christ understands our trials and temptations because He was Himself tempted? Was Jesus a man? Half God, Half man? Purely God?

Take this cup away: what Messiah really meant.

The laughable interpretations of why the Venerable Christ became vulnerable and cried, "My God, My God, Why have you forsaken me?" What did He really say and mean?

Messiah as the model Shepherd and Bridegroom.

Cerebral versus spiritual understanding of the Godhead.

The gifts of arts and science, granted by Adonai, are ways of helping mankind unravel some of the mysteries of the universe, but not its Creator, who is Beyond Understanding.

How does it feel to be on your own and rejected?

The desire not to be saved.

Have you received Immanuel, God's Gift? And more.

This I Believe

I am unapologetic and uncompromising in my belief that the Holy Bible, the entire collection, is *the* Immutable Word of Adonai. It is *the* Foundation and Scaffolding for constructing and sustaining the believer's faith in Yeshua Messiah. Unlike empiricist theologians, we do not need to employ the reasoning of science to establish or bolster our unflinching faith in the Triune God. We may escort people to the doorway into the Holy of Holies, but they themselves, of their own volition, must knock on the door and, when it opens, walk through. We are, as Apostle Paul would say, persuaded that God waits excitedly to reveal Himself to those who seek Him with all their heart. We know beyond every doubt and proclaim unequivocally that the Word of God is Truth, even when we fail to find empirical bases for our belief. As A. W. Tozer once advised, "We should never retreat before truth simply because we can't explain it."

Target Audience

I offer this book to everyone who is humble and open-minded, who reads thoughtfully, who stops to meditate on God's True Nature and our relationship to Him, and who already believes in Him and His Holy Word or else remains open to believing in Him and the Holy Bible as more than a history book or a compilation of folk tales by daydreaming zealots. I invite everyone to study its central teaching: the Ultimate Message of the Torah-Tenach, the *Old Testament*, and the Brit Chadasha, the *New Testament*, is the Essentiality of Jesus the Messiah to our Redemption and Everlasting Life. He and the Holy Trinity are One and the Same. We refer to the Three as the Father, the Son, and the Holy Spirit, but They are Inseparable. I, as a fallible human who cannot know the Unknowable, have made every effort to describe the Nature of God as He Actually Is, not as I desire Him to be, for He Is already Perfection Itself. Everyone who feels qualified, as above, or who desires to feel qualified is invited to travel with us as we consider and celebrate Adonai's True Nature.

Not being an academic theologian, I do not make lengthy, complex theological arguments, splitting hairs about, for example, exactly where and when Jesus shed the sins of the world that He had taken upon Himself. I speak plainly in the language of everyday people. Guided by the Holy Spirit, available to all of us, I present the simple Truths *sola scriptura*, believing that Spiritual Truths are revealed only in the Holy Scriptures.

The book is designed to help Christians who are honestly seeking spiritual illumination in order to know the Creator and His creation but who perhaps have sidetracked the most important Truths. I hope that the information and reverent perspective will deepen the believing follower's relationship with the Messiah and reveal the foolishness and dangers of accusing God rather than trusting Him. Many who have accused Him have done so from ignorance rather than arrogance. Mindful learning transforms ignorance into knowledge and wisdom.

It is my prayer that, somewhere between the covers of this book, God's Truth will confront those who now accuse Him of fallibility and will present them with the choice to retract their accusatory statements against God, confess their sins, perform acts of contrition, accept God's Forgiveness, and resolve never again to accuse Him. As always with our Divine Father, such choices are ours to make.

Joining the Choir

When in the face of assorted difficulties, especially those that forestall efforts to resolve them, people naturally feel forsaken, first by other people, then by God, or vice versa. Many tend to forgive fellow humans involved yet, directly or indirectly, accuse Almighty God, **Yahweh** Adonai, of circuitously abandoning them instead of resolving their difficulties or preventing their problems in the first place. It is not uncommon to see men and women shake their fists in the face of God, asking Him why He is silent in response to their prayers or why He allowed such and such to happen: "We trusted you, and now you have failed us." Under the intense squeeze of their unresolved circumstances, they subsequently find Him guilty of equivocation, of speaking out of both sides of his mouth. The accusers' claim is usually that God has abandoned them after He promised that He would never leave us or forsake us. They produce what appears to be a salient reason to propose that God abandons us when we need Him most. Are you one of the accusers of God? In some sense, all men and women accuse God of falling short of His promises. Read on and see how.

Drenched by unsavory personal experiences, "victims" have proffered that it was God's passive, even nonchalant, attitude toward their supplications that facilitated their disappointments and disasters. Well-meaning clergy, laity, theologians, philosophers, and mystics have written extensively, and preachers have preached widely, humanizing God and inadvertently teaching billions of unsuspecting believers that God cannot be trusted. They do not intentionally distort the Inerrant Word of God, but by teaching errant conventional doctrines—for instance, the one holding that God forsook Christ at Calvary ("Why hast Thou forsaken me?"). The trusting congregants complete the picture: if God is capable of turning His back on His Son, certainly He must turn His back on us ordinary human beings. Some even find the self-righteous gall to edit scriptural verses and come up with such misinterpretations as I saw in a popular journal: "He who did not spare his son after the heart-rending groaning at Gethsemane and Calvary could not be trusted to do less to, or more for mankind." Sounds like a verse from the Holy Bible, but it is not. One purpose of the book is to help readers discern the difference between God's Word and insidious misrepresentations.

Not Just an Attempt to Defend God

Ridiculous, isn't it, that the Almighty God, Creator of all things, has been maligned so universally, if unintentionally, that Christians who reject the charges must stand up and set the record straight. In this book, indeed I stand as a defender of Adonai against the long string of frivolous, vicious, unconscionable accusations against Him. I invite you to join the holy crusade. He Is Perfect! In the best of worlds, God would need no defenders. At various times in human history, true believers have sensed the need and stood up, so that people might again see the Almighty as the True Godhead. Such men and women, through their songs, poems, prose, and speeches, embrace and celebrate God's Sovereignty, Omnipotence, Omniscience, and Omnipresence as the Epitome of Goodness, Justice, and Worthiness. They proclaim that there is no other god—only Adonai. Their harmonious voices resound: *"Adonai yimloch l'olam va-ed"* ("The Lord our God will reign forever and ever."). And we all sing, "The Lord our God is good. His loving kindness and mercy endure forever. Amen."

Who Wants to Be an Advocate for God?

Above, I acknowledge that most Christians caught up in the gradual universal trend to elevate mankind and humanize God, viewing Him, alas, as fallible—are good, well-meaning people. However, believers must always be mindful that, just as the serpent tempted Eve, Satan constantly seeks openings through which to slither. Of course, the devil is no threat to Adonai, who is Omnipotent. Nor is the prince of darkness a threat to true believers who put their trust in the Lord and follow Him. Once the Spirit fills us, there is no room for Satan. He is a vanquished foe. But, the evil one nonetheless can penetrate the hearts and minds of wavering believers, tempting them, for example, to believe the popular notion that God is like us and therefore fallible, therefore capable of forsaking us. Followers who have put their trust in God and His Immutable Word are protected. The problem is that most people are not listening or hearing. Their ears are blocked by the same calluses that shield their hearts from the Truth. As my son once proposed, "Let us all in ceaseless, humble supplication, callous our knees and elbows, and not our hearts; yet if our hearts must be, let [them] be layered with the Word of the holy God who alone is the sure shield against the wiles of our determined foe."

Even though God does not really need or depend on us for anything, it would be an honor to be found worthy and to be used by God to help bring about the fulfillment of His desires here on earth. Feeling this empowerment, I am compelled to share my fears, my burdens, God's revelation, and His Heart with those who desire to be released from the shackles of Satan. After all, the Messiah's Great Commission does command us to "preach, teach, and reach all people with the Gospel (the Good News) of Adonai's Kingdom.

In writing this book, I boldly, but humbly, join many others in the Choir of the Lamb, performing the honorable, if perilous, task of holding up the banner of the Almighty God—as another feeble voice in the song of worship of Adonai, celebrating Yeshua, the Venerable One and God's promised Salvation, our Redemption from the kingdom of darkness. I, and my invaluable team, could not have accomplished the task, were it not for empowerment by the Holy Spirit. It is my prayer and hope that the book counts.

It is Coarse, Direct, and Didactic.

The book has not been written in conventional twenty-first-century form, whatever that is. I remain mindful of human diversity ranging from relatively unschooled to highly educated. To foster universal understanding, I employ accessible language and methodology, rather than esoteric theological jargon. Although I did earn a doctoral degree from a respected American university, I am not grounded in the mind-set and lingo of contemporary seminarians. Also, I was "called" to write this book, under the instruction of the Holy Spirit, over a number of years having heard a persistent "Voice" within. I honor the "Voice" that has revealed what to say and how to say it. The book is didactic, providing pertinent information and teaching core lessons about the Nature of God and our Ideal relationship with Him.

Reminiscence

Besides hearing the "call" of God's persistent "Voice," my wife and I have lived through many complex personal experiences that, ultimately, have inspired and smoothed the writing process. Connie recalls,

> We have passed through life's frightening channels and labyrinths populated by men and women with the penchant to abandon their kind. We have been pushed, sometimes gagged and dragged, to brinks of mind-bending and

heart-numbing experiences. We know what it is like to be or feel forsaken. Days on our knees and nights on sweat—and tear-soaked pillows. Hours and weeks spent meditating on the Holy Writ and supplicating Adonai seemed to have fallen short of impressing Jehovah Jireh (Adonai, our provider). We even thought that heaven, hell, and earth had finally found a point of convergence, an agreement that we would be tortured, forsaken, and then destroyed . . . I am sure that many of our readers have been or are presently there—the wilderness of testing. For those, we can only say, stay strong, be resolute, and exercise your faith, which comes by hearing and believing the Word of God, for the Lord your God will definitely turn to your page; yes, in His time.

I hope you now see why I am passionate about the topic of being forsaken. What is not easily reconciled is the fact that neither I, nor Connie, is indicting Adonai, but rather, perhaps surprisingly, defending Him. Our ardent and sometimes stinging reactions, especially to the inference that God behaves like humans and forsakes His children, testifies to our monumental conviction—inspired and cushioned by the Word of God.

It is perhaps understandable that, when we rationalize our human proclivity to forsake others, we also extend this human fragility to Adonai. But doing so is not unlike blaspheming against the Holy Spirit, an offense, which, according to the Holy Scriptures, cannot be atoned for! Brethren, the Omnipotent Jehovah Elohim is not man, even though He walked the earth as if He were a man and still willingly condescends to reason with us. He is the Creator of all things, seen and unseen. He is God the Father, who is the Son of God and God the Son. He is the Holy Spirit. Venerate Him, and Him Alone!

What the Author Has Tried to Do

In listening to my son, Tobechukwu's song, *"Your Infinitude"* in his debut album, I am awestruck at the Infinity of my God.

> "This one I can't understand / This one I can't comprehend / Your Infinitude
>
> This one I cannot grasp / To this there is no math / Your Infinitude
>
> What do I say to a God Who has no beginning? / I am a child of a God Who has no end
>
> From everlasting to everlasting You are God. From everlasting You will be the same"

One of the most important and consistent efforts I have made is to present evidence of God's *infinitude*. For He is Omniscient, Omnipotent, and Omnipresent. I argue robustly that God is not human and, therefore, does not grope for and stumble over His Word[s]. The blessed One is Omniscient and, therefore, Knows His Master Plan from beginning to end.

He is Immutable and, therefore, does not change His Mind. He did not create Eve from one of Adam's ribs and then decide to use a leg bone instead. He Executes His Plan step by step, without conflict, confusion, or collision.

After dispassionately witnessing all accusations against Him, even after mankind's attempts through the ages to humanize Him, the Lord remains Unscathed, Unadulterated, Immutable. He is as Purely Divine now as He was before "the beginning," and will remain so after "the end." *Baruch Adonai.* Blessed is the Lord, our God!

Active Participants in God's Work

To qualify as an active participant in this exercise, I advise that we all hearken personally to the Holy Scriptures because every word in the Word is from the Lord. Though the speaker of the words may sometimes sound mortal, even corporeal, as in some of the utterances of Solomon in his Songs, they are still from the Lord. The predicament arises when the Lord's good intentions and purposes are lost, misconceived, misinterpreted, mistaken, and misapplied. It is vitally important to understand that some of the teachings of the Holy Bible are so steeped in spirituality, metaphors, and allegories that their meanings are hard to discern but, indeed, can be deciphered through the illumination of the seeker by the Holy Spirit, the true writer of the Scriptures. God's explanations or revelations of His Word come to us in several ways: dreams, visions, trances, "heard" inner messages of knowledge and wisdom, prophecies, and the like.

Adonai Speaks All Languages and Anoints All Available Vessels

Some students of the Holy Bible have chased after the hidden nuggets in the Word through intense study of ancient languages: Aramaic, Hebrew, Greek, Yiddish, Latin, etc. They hope to strain out all confusions and discover "that thing" that makes a word *the* Word of Adonai. As a messianic believer, I completely agree that all Christians need to sit under an enlightened rabbi in order to hear the ancient truths as documented in the native language of Jesus. But does it mean that God cannot speak all other languages to non-linguists and lay students of the Holy Bible? The clear answer is no, because God does continually speak to "ordinary" people who do not have formal education. When we fellowship with such men and women, "something" confirms spiritually that we are in the presence of God's anointed servant. The anointing—yes, that's what makes the difference. Remember Peter at the Feast of the Pentecost? The outpouring of Adonai's Spirit and everyone at the gathering hearing Peter in their own native language? Also keep in mind the conversion of three thousand men (not counting women and children) to faith in Jesus Messiah. Is that not confounding? That is true anointing!

All Revelations Are Equally Important, but . . .

Again, all revelations are important, but some may seem and actually be more vital, therefore deserving immediate, sustained prayerful meditation, diligent investigation, appropriate documentation, provable interpretation, and urgent dissemination. Those can only be done outside the reaches of the flesh and beyond the relentless, all-devouring flame of secular humanism. Accomplishing such tasks is only possible under the constant influence and guidance of the Holy Spirit. The outcome may not be popular. But a revelation's authenticity and acceptance does not have to depend on the endorsement of a majority of Gentiles, Jews, presidents, senators, councils, committees, popes, priests, pastors, rabbis, prophets. Its intended results should not be controlled or limited by the dissenting voices of some theologians, philosophers, existentialist–New Agers, mystics, or any other so-called experts on the perverted universal spiritual consciousness.

Subtle Stronghold of Satan: the Hocus-Pocus

God Himself does not need exonerating, for He is Perfect. The book's implicit rationale is to free mankind from the hidden stronghold of the enemy: the tendency for mankind to view and judge God as if He were human with human flaws. A close look at the everyday "pilgrim's progress" through life reveals a subtle to violent systematized erosion of Adonai's Attributes, in mankind's determination to strip God of His

Divinity. In a frenzied Satan-influenced fantasy, we have focused the floodlight on Messiah, Jesus (Immanuel), God incarnate, in borrowed flesh, dwelling among His people. To get a clear shot, the crosshairs are centered on Christ's "humanity": allegedly His vulnerability, the "fact" that He had a physical body and was "tempted in every possible way," just like any of us. The other half of the quotation, "but He did not sin," escapes the eye and mind of the evil minded. Mankind gradually targets Christ's Divinity and Holiness, with an expected end product in mind: reducing Him to the status of any ordinary man prone to making mistakes, regretting decisions made, prevaricating, and making adjustments to original plans.

At the end of the hocus-pocus, after reducing God's size and adjusting His qualities to benefit mankind's intention, what is produced is a god who would eventually need men, women, and angels to rescue him when he is in trouble. Let us be wise and know that this powerless, quibbling, equivocating god is not Elohim, but one made by mankind in mankind's likeness.

The Rebirth of Classical Ideology

This tendency to blaspheme God and therefore commit heterodoxy was inspired by the interest of modern mankind in Greco-Roman culture, a powerful stimulant, which, among other things, encouraged a new kind of liberty: mankind's independence from God. Inclination to this ideology gradually eroded reverential fear of the Almighty God and the pursuit of godly wisdom. In its wake, that culture left the most adversarial antichrist sentiment called secular humanism, an ideology that is abundantly manifest in modernist and postmodernist proclivities, making a powerful impression on the 21st-century church. Under its powerful spell, we have measured ourselves against ourselves, established ourselves as the "measure of all things," and, to our own damnation, foolishly deified ourselves. In the process, perniciously, we have humanized our vision of God. Some of us may have heard that line before from the very lips of Satan (Isaiah 14:14). Not that mankind can, in actuality, strip Adonai of Divinity, but we can be led to believe so in our demon-infested imagination.

Thinking that we are wise, we have become foolish, so much so that we see ourselves as a kind of god and God as a kind of man—a limited earthling.

Getting Ready for Battle

In the course of evidence collection, extensive "visits were paid and discussions held" with the Prophets of old and some not so old. Yes, convincing evidence would be needed to "vindicate" God, in the face of His accusers, and present Him as the Faultless Creator of the universe. Connie and I, as many before us, stand in the witness box to testify in God's defense, because the charges, that He prevaricates and consequently abandons or forsakes His children, carry cosmic repercussions. Considering the weightiness of the "case," prospective friendly witnesses must be full of the Holy Spirit and armed with evidence, both empirical and spiritual.

Given the antagonists' determination to defame Adonai, we defenders of God need air-tight evidence and testimony to prevent being shot down by the horde of antagonistic secular humanist theologians, philosophers, and their nefarious crony-attorneys.

Who Is on the Lord's Side?

Surprisingly, the roster is impressive even though most voices come from the very distant past, distinct echoes of unwavering conviction. Among those who testify to Adonai's *Omniness and Infinitude* are Abraham, Isaac and Jacob, Job, Moses, Joshua, King David, the wise King Solomon, Prophets Isaiah, Jeremiah, and Ezekiel, the Blessed Virgin Mary, the Apostles, Aiden Tozer, Leonard Ravenhill, Billy Graham, Oral Roberts, and a multitude of others. For instance, Novatian, a man not well known in 21st-century Christian circles, grappling with the issue of God's Omniness and Infinitude in the 3rd century, said, in a famous treatise on the Trinity, that "every possible statement that can be made about God expresses some possession or virtue of God rather than God Himself. The conception of God as He is can only be grasped in one way—by thinking of Him as a being whose attributes and greatness are beyond our power of understanding, or even of thought." Hence our third son's name, *Chidiomimi*, from the Nigerian Igbo language, which translates as "Adonai is Unfathomable"—Very Deep.

Why am I so feverish concerning Adonai's Omniness and Infinitude and, therefore, His Infallibility? Here is the cut-and-dried answer: if a prosecuting attorney can discredit just one word of a witness, the individual is found guilty of lying, even if he or she has told the truth. Just a shadow of a doubt, and the entire case is lost. In the same way, my brethren, if the accusers of God could make one of their many fantasies stick, the entire Holy Bible would become an extension of Grimm's fairy tales. Such will not happen, I am confident, but should God's every Scriptural Word come into question, before long, the detractors could accomplish their purpose: not only to humanize God, but to destroy Him in the eyes of mankind. After all, a desperate and frustrated philosopher in the very recent past, declared God dead.

What I am saying is simply that, should God be found to have equivocated even once, then the accusations that He forgets and forsakes us will, for so many, be set in stone, thereby establishing the erroneous interpretation of ". . . Why have you forsaken me?" as accurate!

Repetitious on Purpose

Sensitive to, and nearly fanatical about, the central issues, that God does not lie and God does not forsake His children, I establish the main points and then re-emphasize them from time to time throughout the book. This practice may distract some readers, but I intentionally seek to ensure that readers remain mindful of our essential purpose: to *validate* God's Word; to *eradicate* heretical fallacies; to *vindicate* God's Omniness and Infallibility in the face of accusations accumulating since the fall of Eve and Adam; and to *light* the path of escape from sure destruction awaiting those who choose to shun the Light.

Repeated essential themes, periodic reminders, are intended to engage and re-engage the reader with core issues in a rhythm that is like a song's refrain, permeating the reader's consciousness, sub-consciousness, and super-consciousness. Prone to forgetfulness, as St. James said in his epistle of exhortation, we look at their faces in the mirror, but immediately forget what they looked like as soon as their backs are turned to the mirror. Repetition serves as a safeguard against spiritual amnesia. The Holy Bible itself contains numerous instances where Adonai repeats the same command, just as the same highway-safety signs are placed periodically to remind us, for example, of the speed limit.

Preamble

Theme Music: Adonai Does Not, Did Not, and Will Never Forsake the Righteous

Abundant evidence and testimonies from both the living and the dead, who now live with Christ, demonstrate conclusively that if someone lied, it was not God; if someone equivocated, it was not God; and if anyone forsook anyone, it was mankind that forsook God. It was mankind that forsook the Messiah when He hung on the cross, not Adonai, His Father. It would be oxymoronic if "God forsook God." It would be tantamount to His forsaking Himself, for God the Father, God the Son, and God the Holy Spirit are Three in One! They are One and the Same! Furthermore, the Divine Mission of Jesus the Messiah on earth was to save each and every righteous earthling. God's forsaking of Jesus would be tantamount to forsaking the righteous. Adonai would never forsake the righteous. He said to Joshua, "Moses my servant is dead. Now, you and all these people, get ready to cross the Jordan River into the land that I am about to give to them . . . As I was with Moses, so I will be with you. I will never leave you nor forsake you" (Joshua 1:2–5). He did not forsake him, has not forsaken anyone, and will not ever forsake those who put their trust in Him.

Let us open our eyes and see the enemy's ploy, the very old tactic of "giving the dog a bad name to justify its liquidation." If Adonai, as He did, promised not to forsake His children, He meant exactly that. He said, "I will protect you, I will be with you even till the end of times." Friends, Adonai Keeps His Word by Performing It. Let us all continue to pray with and for the faith to trust Him completely. He will not fail us!

Prerequisites for Receiving Adonai's Protection and Provision

There are clear prerequisites to qualify for His Eternal Protection and Provision. "Be careful to obey all the Law my servant Moses gave to you, do not turn from it, to the right or to the left, that you may be successful wherever you go. Do not let this book of the law depart from your mouth; meditate upon it day and night, that you may be careful to do everything written in it. Then, you will be prosperous and successful" (Joshua 1: 6–8). God did not, does not, and will never, forsake those who believe in and practice righteousness according to the Word.

Obedience is God's Beloved Song

Mankind's relationship with God has progressively soured over the decades as a result of an insidious groundswell of seemingly glamorous, highly toxic, postmodernist attitudes. We have continually drifted away from the covenants that God made with us. Worse still is the perplexing but persistent disobedience of the Commandments that Almighty Adonai set before us with a command: 'Be careful to obey all the Law . . . Then, you will be prosperous and successful" (Joshua 1:5).

Twenty-first-century secular-humanist theologians teach that the Grace of God has overcome God's laws. If they were right, God would be shortsighted, would He not, instead of Omniscient. If He were Omniscient, He would have Foreknown that the Grace He had Planned to Provide would eradicate the Law that He had Provided, rendering Him a changeable liar. Brethren, does not God Know All Things? Has He not Known Them from the beginning? Adonai said to Prophet Jeremiah, "Before I formed you in your mother's womb, I foreknew you" (Jeremiah 1:5). Of course He did! Let us not be led astray by wayward theologians or well-meaning neighbors!

Obeying His Law must be the most important act of willingness by mankind to work for and walk with the Creator, for again and again Adonai instructed, "These Commandments that I give you today are to be upon your heart. Impress them on your children, talk about them when you sit at home, and when you walk along the road, when you lie down and when you get up. Tie them as symbols on your hands, and bind them on your foreheads. Write them on the door frames of your houses and on your gates" (Deuteronomy 6:6).

King Solomon counsels, "My son, do not forget my teachings, but keep my commands in your heart" (Proverbs 3:1). Apostle Paul, who in many ways could be designated as the New Testament equivalent of Solomon, reminds us that "keeping God's Commands is what counts" (1 Corinthians 7:19). At the end of his treatise chronicled in Ecclesiastes, King Solomon, a man who enjoyed the unparalleled gift of wisdom and understanding from God, advocates, "Now all has been heard, here is the conclusion of the matter; Fear God and keep His Commandments, for this is the whole duty of man." All I can add is *Amen*.

Additionally, King Solomon pleads that we trust the Lord with all our heart, to lean not on our own understanding; that in all our ways we should acknowledge God, and only then, will He, God, make our path straight (Proverbs 3). He seems to be advising that we should believe in God with all that we are and all that we have; after all, that is why true Christians are called *believers* and those who are not are called *unbelievers*. But can we, and should we, truly believe in something or someone we do not know or understand? Is it possible for two to agree to work in harmony if they fundamentally have divergent views and rules? Can we yoke a horse to an elephant and expect unity?

A. W. Tozer cautions that "any belief that does not command the man who holds it is not real belief: it is pseudo belief only." True belief in Adonai, belief that emotes from an understanding heart, brings about worship and praise. And that is why King Solomon proclaims, "Guard your heart, for it is the well spring of life" (Proverbs 4:23).

What Parts of the B*ook of the Law* or the *Commandments* Are Written upon Our Hearts

Yes, upon our *hearts*. And what of them have we impressed upon our children? The answers are expected to be as diverse as there are peoples of different backgrounds, dogmas, doctrines, and experiences. However, generally speaking, mankind has consciously or inadvertently challenged all of them and faulted a goodly number. Have people of the world not installed the constitutions of their nations over the Commandments of God? And have they not vigorously taught their children to do the same? Let us be mindful of what is happening globally. Politicians, flirting with and drooling over the electorate in hopes of clutching a leadership position, amend or erase God's Commandments. In their quest to satisfy the people's whims, they will say and promise anything to their adoring, myopic, hard-of-hearing constituents, often profaning the very Name of God and damning His Commandments. Alas, the countries of the world are, for the most part, governed by slick politicos, who borrow illusionism from Houdini and Mesmer and oratorical mastery from Pericles and Sir Winston Churchill. Whatever happened to righteousness?

Have church leaders and their drifting flock fared any better? Categorically no! "Thou shall not" has become a mere suggestion that, at will, is disregarded. Siamak-David, a believing Christian and follower of Yeshua Messiah, put it this way: "Christ instructs that we pray without ceasing, the contemporary Christian edits it and comes up with 'Play without ceasing'" Great rhyme, terrible affront! The illustration may sound unsophisticated, but, brethren, that is exactly what we have done with the Word, even the Commandments of God. There used to be ten of them, but mankind has sacrificed some to lustful impulses. Results are varied, anything from nine Commandments to none at all. The divinely inspired wisdom of the sages through the ages, the Commands and Precepts of the Ancient of Days, have all been cast off as obsolete, not absolute, and only fit for the 21st century mausoleum of derelict religious *objets d'art*.

Yes, to many, the Word of Adonai is relevant no more. The phrase "no more" connotes that the Word "once was" relevant. We have learned to use the Word of God as crutches, which we hastily discard as soon as we achieve our desired, usually mundane, objective. The voice of Shakespeare's Cassius echoes from the past: "Lowliness is the young ambitious ladder, whereby the climber upward turns his face, but as soon as he attains the point desired, he looks down at the base degrees by which he did ascend" (*Julius Caesar*). In our minds we think we have fooled Adonai, but we must be careful of our foolishness, because, as Apostle Paul wrote to Timothy, "The sins of many men get to the seat of judgment ahead of them, but the sins of others come behind them" (1 Timothy 5:24). Whatever we sow, that shall we also reap—a hundred fold or more.

The Law: Kinship between the *Torah* (Old Testament) and the *Brit Chadasha* (New Testament)

To ensure that modern-day proponents of the so-called new dispensation do not create a chasm between the *Torah/Tenach* (Old Testament) and the *Brit Chadasha* (New Testament), the *Ancient of Days* manifested, in Christ, His Omniscience and maintained consistency in what He spoke. The *Torah* foreshadows the Brit Chadasha, and the Brit Chadasha fulfills the Torah. For example, He employs the same words in the New Testament to highlight His unwavering demand of complete obedience from mankind: "If you love me, keep my commandments," for "how can you call me Lord, when you do not obey my commands? With your lips you praise me, but your hearts are distant from me." This is how Matthew recorded it: "These people draw near to me with their mouth and honor me with their lips, but their heart is far from Me" (Matthew 15:8).

Evil men and women with dark intentions have been at work, constructing an impassable divide between the Old and New Testaments. The Old, which they claim has passed away, represents Law and Judgment, while the New, which represents Grace, overflows with freedom from the Law. As they frantically grasp for straws, hoping to prop up their ailing faith in God, they profusely quote Saint Paul out of context. Let us most lovingly tell the foxes that their deep holes will not protect them on the day of the Lord's wrath.

A Jamaican reggae singer, Peter Tosh, bellowed, "O sinner man, where you gonna run to all on that day? . . . the sea will be boiling . . . the rock will be melting . . . all on that day."

Concerned believers are constantly asking why their hearts are distant from the Lord our God and why they are going through the painful up-and-down road of life. There are many reasons why life is a climb up Mount Everest and a sudden descent into the Grand Canyon, but hearken to the voice of Adonai. It is possible to hear the Lord respond from His Holy Mountain:

> My Word is not upon your hearts. You have not impressed them on your children; neither have you talked about them when you sit at home, and when you walk on along the road, when you lie down and when you get up. You have refused to

tie them as symbols on your hands, and bind them on your foreheads. Moreover, I cannot find them written on the door frames of your houses and on your gates. You have hidden My Word because you now prostitute with strange gods and goddesses, to whom you now offer your putrefied sacrifices.

To seek recompense for such disobedience, most people roam the mind's inner halls of past dreams, traumas, sicknesses, deaths. While it is commendable to search out causes and effects, people do not suffer simply because of disobedient acts. When true believers in and followers of the Word stray into disobedience, they know in their hearts that, if they confirm their trust in God, confess, and ask for forgiveness, Salvation awaits them. In others, however, ignorance of the Word beclouds the heart and mind, especially in times of tribulation. They feel distant from God, perhaps even forsaken. Some blame God. Lacking the ability to discriminate, for example, between a test by god and a temptation by Satan, they find themselves plunging into the chasm and knowing no way to survive.

In the Pursuit of Freedom and Happiness, Obey God's Commands

Mankind has vigorously pursued freedom and happiness and, in the process, lost life's most important, enduring, sustaining elements: Freedom from evil and the Loving Embrace of Adonai, Yeshua, and the Holy Spirit. Only those who choose to be righteous achieve that Freedom and that Embrace. The choice to be righteous is available to all living earthlings. When we choose to believe in and follow the Messiah, the Son of the Living God, when we regularly meditate prayerfully on the Word, continually exploring and affirming our faith and our understanding, when we regularly confess our sins and seek God's Forgiveness, we are declared righteous and granted Salvation. Those of us who are righteous follow God's Commands willingly because we are in agreement with them.

Fractional agreement, semi-obedience, may look like obedience, but it is not. It is disobedience. Considering all of human history, imagine how many tombstones might have read,

> Here's lies the Jones family, who thought they deserved to enter the Kingdom of Heaven and live there forever in Love and Serenity. They almost made it. But the gatekeeper, St. Peter, turned away all but little Alice.

> "The rest of you," he said," lived pretty decent lives, for which I commend you, but you all hedged your bets on some of God's Commandments. You know the rules.

> For example, Harold, all too often you allowed yourself to be preoccupied with your gambling addiction. You worshipped gambling as if it were a god. Sorry, but that's how it goes.

Same with the rest of you. You know what you thought and did.

But, you, Alice—God welcomes you here. Despite your family's backsliding, you have lived your short life filled with the Spirit, devoted to God, your church, and your community. Bless you, child! You are truly one of the righteous ones!

The Way of the Lord is Good and Just!"

Perfect Obedience, Semi-obedience, and Complete Disobedience

When the Venerable Yeshua HaMaschiach (Jesus the Messiah) asked His Father to "forgive them for they know not what they do," He was not only asking forgiveness for the actions that took place at Golgotha; He meant forgiveness for all mankind's acts of insubordination, from the time of Adam and Eve. It is safe to assume that most people who ended up disobeying God started out with honest intentions—the desire and resolve to walk with Adonai. Unfortunately, good intentions are not good enough. We must make real our good intentions by acting in accord with them, so that in our daily lives we affirm our being in total agreement with God.

Let us review Messiah's plea, from the cross, to His Father. He was specific on the reason why He pled: ". . . for they do not understand what they do." What did they do? They crucified the Son of Righteousness, the incarnation of

Adonai, the Sacrifice offered for the Atonement of their sins. But that was then. Yes, they did not understand, but now we do, and because of the knowledge that has been granted us, God expects us—and rightly so—to make mindful, godly choices in our lives, moment to moment, as an ongoing spiritual practice. Godly beliefs produce godly actions that produce godly results!

Obedience is Better than Sacrifice

To assist prospective Christian believers in navigating away from the brinks of partial obedience, let us recall the repercussions of some well-known rebellious actions: Adam and Eve flirted with Satan and traded eternal bliss for momentary delight. Moses, blinded by rage, pressured by the bickering of his countrymen, smote the rock instead of, as the Lord had commanded, speaking to it, thus bringing upon himself the wrath of God. Aaron, the chief priest, sculpted the golden calf, an action that cost him his seat on the "flight" into the Promised Land. Samson's flirtation with the delightful but dangerous temptress Delilah makes a great sermon on how not to dialogue with Satan. King David's rendezvous with Uriah's wife brought about the conspiracy that took her husband's life. The wisest and richest of them all, King Solomon, in spite of God's repeated warnings, married pagan women, who introduced him to contrary spirits. Prophet Jonah preferred going to Tarshish than, by God's command, to Nineveh. Uzzah, in his great zeal to protect the Ark of Adonai, against His commands, put his hand on the ark, earning for himself the death penalty (2

Samuel 6:6). In the throes of schizophrenia and impatience, King Saul performed the duties of a high priest. Additionally, contrary to God's command to decimate the Amalekites, King Saul spared the lives of King Agag and the choicest flocks of the Amalekites, sparking Samuel's decisive five-word rebuke: "Obedience is better than sacrifice."

It is refreshing and faith strengthening to know that the only One who Obeyed Absolutely and Offered the Perfectly Unblemished Sacrifice was the Incomparable, Immeasurable, Immutable Messiah, the Venerable Jesus Christ. May His Glorious Name be praised forever! Amen.

Chapter 1

THE COMMISSION

My Fear of Serving

I woke several times in the course of last night, as I did yesterday, and at different times, many days and years before, and was finally awakened by a persistent, throbbing headache. It was not the discomfort that held me captive but rather an importunate vision that shadowed me and increasingly overwhelmed me. The hot red finger appearing often in my series of visions and dreams had etched a word in my mind and a conviction in my heart and spirit. Yet, it was neither the vision nor the conviction that threatened me, but the mandate that followed them. The paralyzing fear and implicit threat to my earthly existence were legitimate. What I seemed to be hearing as my instruction would go against the established conventions of the twenty-first-century church, to which I was supposed to be delivering God's message. In today's prevalent religious system, doctrines and dogmas are sacred, and those who propose a change, even if commanded by God and therefore veritable, are subject to ostracism. Some are even denounced as heretical.

On their assigned mission, many believing followers of the Venerable Messiah have experienced such threats, which drain human strength, threaten earthly existence, and force pilgrims to lean on the strong arm of God. The sojourner is filled by the sustaining Spirit of Adonai only when his or her knapsack and canteen are empty of bread and water. Only then does the iron heat to brilliant red in the furnace of affliction. Only then does the Master of the Universe shape the metal to His desired use. It was under this Divine Unction that Martin Luther the Reformer renounced all that was renounceable and cried "Sola Scriptura."

Although neither a prophet nor the son of a prophet, merely an unwilling candidate, I, for the first time, surely not in the same league as the prophets, genuinely understood why Moses, Isaiah, Jeremiah, Ezekiel, and many other true men and women were paralyzed by trepidation when God commissioned and anointed them. Can you see the marked difference in the reactions of those whom Adonai appointed to minister in the past and the reactions of those today who are appointed by mere mortals? God's appointees protested their assignments, flooding His Throne with tears and logical reasons why they did not feel worthy or capable. They were spiritually discerning, able to foreknow what perils would endanger their paths, what hordes of hellhounds would dog them wherever they went. They protested their appointments, knowing the consequences. They also accepted and embraced their appointments, no matter what the personal cost. Internal struggle raged between their mundane desire to be accepted by humankind and their transcendent desire to serve the Almighty.

Those many of us who live to serve God, do we not, at one time or another, consider restructuring or rewording a thought or message because we dread people's reaction to us more than we revere and fear Adonai? What an absurdity! What a contradiction! Such paradoxes prevail because our hearts are desperately wicked, says the Lord of Hosts, and, from time to time, we, even as believing Christians, look away from the Redeemer and cast our eyes upon the impending storms of human circumstances. It took the Omniscient Spirit of God to forge the spaghetti spines of men such as Martin Luther the Reformer and Martin Luther King, Jr., the Marcher into spines of steel. Jehovah empowered them to perform unprecedented services despite their fears and doubts. Likewise, the spirit of Adonai forged the conviction and courage of John the Immerser. He dared to rebuke the powerful Herod the Great for his many sins. As well, he rebuked Herod's granddaughter Herodias for declaring herself divorced from her first husband, Herod II, while he still lived, so she could marry another man, Herod Antipas, thus becoming guilty of adultery. It is the absence of this indispensible and vital dynamic Godly essence that causes contemporary clergy, laity, and politicians to speak selectively and cautiously when confronted with questions of morality, virtue, and especially the nature and expectations of God, Christ, and the Holy Spirit.

God's course for me of agonizing nights and morning headaches has enabled me to realize that when the Spirit that transformed such men as John the Baptist possesses a man or woman, the possessed one dies to self, the world, and lust; is resurrected; is transformed, renewed, regenerated; is endowed and anointed by the Holy Spirit to live again. But this time, it is not he or she that lives within that body. It is the venerable Master, Jesus the Messiah, capable of so much more than was previously imaginable. Through God's grace, I have come to realize how men like A. W. Tozer, Leonard Ravenhill, and many other true prophets, preachers, and servants of God lived and ministered as they did. They were possessed by the All-Knowing Spirit of God, and they died without being duly appreciated or memorialized. Such happens when God's chosen ones take up the cross, deny themselves, and live by their transcendent love for and obedience to Adonai, no matter the cost, even to their parents, brothers and sisters, spouses, and children.

Some Good Recent Prophets Among Us

A. W. Tozer, writing the foreword for his friend Leonard Ravenhill's book, said that "such a man was likely to be drastic, radical, sometimes even violent, and the curious crowd that gathered to watch him work would soon brand him as extreme, fanatical, negative. And in a sense, they were right. He was single-minded and severe, fearless, and these were the qualities the circumstances demanded. He shocked some, frightened others, and alienated not few, but he knew who had called him and what he was sent to do. His ministry was geared to the emergency, and that fact marked him out as different, a man apart".

When measured against the conventional concepts of success, even around Christian circles, these men would be rated paupers, many having died in penury. They did not siphon millions of dollars from congregations, or amass personal wealth through the sale of books written for the wrong reasons, or through the sale of fake holy relics from the Holy Land. True servants of Adonai refuse to do these abominable things, even when they have compelling opportunities, because they have become servants to righteousness and have therefore been empowered and overshadowed by Adonai, whose Glorious Name is blessed forever.

Still Struggling With Fear

After a series of epiphanies and other spiritual experiences, I began to understand many things that I had thought I had knowledge of. I had heard about them, but now I had experienced them. What a difference there is between listening to God from afar and hearing God and Him alone deep within me. I embraced the wisdom behind the entire Book of Job and embraced Job himself, the leper, who underwent an ordeal that is unprecedented to become a transparent, honest steward of Jehovah. Here is the nugget in his saga: "Surely I spoke of things that I did not understand, things too wonderful for me to know . . . My ears had heard of you, but now, my eyes have seen you" (Job 42:1–6).

Particular experiences sharpened my resolve and reshaped the course of my life, especially the determination to seek more of the resource from whence I believed the celestial visitors and messages came. My conversion was dramatic from a mere church-going Christian to a radically saved follower of Yeshua. To fully understand the nature of my conversion, kindly picture me in the typical traditional African environment, a culture so powerful that it somehow controls the Christian's desire to let "the old man die and stay dead." Somehow, not unlike the pervasive postmodernist culture especially in the West, it forces the Christian to syncretize traditional religious belief systems with original, authentic Christocentric conviction. (Later in this chapter, I explore the power of this hybrid over "initiates.")

One thing glared in me: I was a reluctant neophyte practitioner constantly struggling with the nature of my double-sided being: traditional African religion on one side of the coin, Christianity on the other side, heavily colored by teachings of the Roman Catholic Church into which I had been born. My dreams were a coagulation of Roman Catholic doctrine and ritual; myths and legends of ancient Greece and Rome, which I guzzled; and very powerful African paganism. Hearing so many loud voices, I ached and struggled to discern which voice was that of God. It was not very long before the most powerful stimulus that I had ever felt pulled me toward Constance, not an abstract word designating the quality of consistency, but rather a young woman, Connie, whom I had met and would later be privileged to marry.

Eating and Drinking Without Satiation

Bible reading and study became my appetizer, main course, side dish, and dessert. The more I drank from the fountain, the more thirsty I became. The more I ate from the loaf, the more hungry I became. My attitude was "Ecce panis intra homo" ("Behold the bread within man"), so I just ate. My eyes were opening, and I was beginning to see beyond looking. My inner man was gradually awakening from a long slumber and desiring nothing more than "seeing His Face, and touching His Grace." The new illumination brought a stream of new visions and trances as well as words of prophecy and knowledge from Pastor Onwuka and the laity concerning Adonai's plan for my life. I? — in God's plan?

Among the more encouraging and strengthening words of Holy Scripture that have freed me from my fear of what mankind might and will do to me is the Prophet Ezekiel's telling of his encounter with Adonai. It is found in chapter 33 of the book that the prophet recorded. Either I imagined that I had this same dialogue with the Almighty or I actually did. Whichever would not surprise me because I admired the prophet Ezekiel even in my dark days of disobedience and rebellion as an unbelieving Christian.

I had no particular desire to rewrite the Ten Commandments, but, in my ignorance, I certainly chipped and cracked the tablets of stone on which they were written. The powerful formative influences in my life persisted: ancient myths and legends, paganism, half-baked truths disseminated by the predominant orthodox churches, dark literature such as Bramm Stoker's "Dracula," many books on the subject of possession, a little bit of transcendental magic, an unprecedented flirtation with the occult clothed and presented as Christian mysticism, and, yes, the list is longer. Lust for demonstrable supernatural power lured me into such practices as breeding vampire bats and scorpions, although, perhaps fortunately, I hated snakes of all sorts. This detestation must have been born of my first impression of the slithering reptile that deceived our first parents in the Garden of Eden. In my determination to cause, or at least contribute to, their extinction, I killed them wherever I saw them, in water wells, in gutters, along my path somewhere. I did not know at the time, that our fight with the adversary of our soul had been, and would remain spiritual; hence "The weapon of our warfare is not carnal."

The Spell of Ezekiel

One of the many Books of the Torah that must have cast a holy spell on me was Ezekiel. It still triggers the urge and challenge to continue prospecting in the Lord's Vineyard, even when human energy is spent. It is no wonder, then, that during my *Rededication at Rosh Pinah,* in Ohio, in the United States, I took the name Ezekiel for my own.

This is what the Lord spoke to me:

> I am sending you to a very religious and intellectual people. They have intensely sought for me, but not with all their hearts, and have written many a great book and spoken great words, words sometimes too high for their understanding. What I ask you to tell them is bitter, but it is my filter that would sift the last chaff from my grains. Their arrogance would rise up because even though they build houses of worship to me, they have sacrificed to Greek and Roman and diverse deities, they muffle their tongues and speak the language of aliens in order to communicate with their gods. They have written many books after their own hearts and minds, they have exalted their knowledge above Me and have led my people astray through them. Great shall be their fall, their destruction, should they fail to hear my chastisement.

So It Is for Every Bearer of God's Message

I was terrified, and the Lord of Glory knew this, so He spoke the same words that He had spoken to Jeremiah, Ezekiel, and many who read this now. See, He never changes. He is Always the Same. He does not stutter or stammer. His Word is clear and simple to understand. "Do not be afraid of them or their words . . . Do not be afraid of what they say, or be terrified by them . . . You must speak my words to them, whether they listen or fail to listen" (Ezekiel 2:6-7). I was being offered the choice of becoming a *watchman*. "But I am not a watchman," I began to respond. "I am only an ordinary man aspiring to understand the deep Mysteries surrounding me, the Universe, and the Godhead."

What I heard in my spirit stunned, stung, and silenced me:

> I culled you out from a heathen environment of people who, though they speak My Name, do not obey My Commands. They have shared their praises among idols made by the hands of ordinary men and sacrificed to strange spirits that inhabit the deeps, covens, and grottoes. But I culled you out for My Name's sake. I taught you to read My Holy Word even though you were a heathen and unrepentant. I told you then, even as I am telling you now, of the many tribulations that you would go through because of Me. You were like the eunuch; you read but understood not what you read. I taught you about Me and My book, and I Baptized you in the Holy Spirit as you sat at your study, wondering about many things concerning My Kingdom. And will you now say, "I am but an ordinary man trying to understand these things"?

Vision, trance, fantasy, epiphany, apparition, or hallucination—I do not know. But something supernatural and extraordinary had taken hold of me. I was a prisoner. There was Someone here that was Spirit; there was a Vivid Message, and a willing and yielding messenger was needed. Was I he, one of the messengers? What qualification do I have? No doubt many, if not all of us, have found ourselves in such circumstances.

It did not matter what I thought. I was completely under the control of this Presence. Then He spoke again. I had heard that Voice, perceived the Fragrance, and experienced the unmistakable *Shalom* of the Glorious One. He was not as patient as He had been earlier on. There was urgency, accusation, threat, and warning encapsulated in every letter of His Word:

> My people have accused Me of lying to them. My Faithfulness has been questioned, and My Divinity and Sovereignty have been eroded in some quarters and destroyed in many. I have been clothed in the robes of Greek and Roman gods and granted the powers of man-beast-gods. They have challenged my Omniness and have put me in space and within time that cannot hold Me or My Glory. Tell My people that I am the Everlasting Infinity even beyond which I exist. Before the beginning I Was, and after the end I Shall Be. Tell My people that the Word that proceeds from My Mouth is Immutable, Ineffable, and Inscrutable. I am not only the Alpha and Omega; I am All That is in Between and All That Is Beyond. So that you would

bear this Revelation, I gave you to your mother. It is a Revelation for all generations. You and many like you who have been sent have kept it to yourselves for too long. I shall wait no more. My anger will boil over upon you and your family, your sons and your daughters, and all the people who have accused Me. You shall be as guilty as they.

I was drenched by my own sweat and tears as I fended off the Lord's fierce anger and accusations. It is difficult to convey what it felt like to be forced to stand in the Presence of Immaculate Purity. Even though mankind has always flirted with the thought of meeting with or seeing Adonai, I questioned my judgment in praying to be in His Actual Presence. Drained of my spirit and ignorant about the heart of this Revelation, I frantically searched my soul for the answer or explanation. What threatened me most was the accusation that I had hoarded the Lord's Revelation. I am aware that the Almighty is blamed for every bad thing that happens. So what expressly is He so enraged about? This must be something of great significance. But what is it?

No matter how hard I tried to untie this cryptic knot, the message remained confusing. I am neither Joseph nor Daniel, who were given the gift of interpretation of dreams and visions. The more I struggled, the more the puzzle enveloped and evaded me. But then—after many days of laboring, a trance, a rewind, reminiscences—there It was. Perhaps I knew all along what Adonai was saying but dared not say it to myself:

Mankind has accused God of prevaricating, the Glorious One is making His Righteous Anger known to us, and He will not judge anyone until all of us have had the chance to hear the Whole Truth.

Our Failure of Vision

As humans, when it comes to seeing God, we are myopic, which is to say, short sighted. Because we cannot "see" God or even "imagine" God, the best we can do is "describe" God by listing attributes with which we are familiar in mankind and nature. We think or say such inadequate descriptors as "God is even more powerful than a tsunami" or "God is even more loving than my grandmother." It is natural and perhaps comforting for us to "imagine" God as being like us. At the same time, it is natural for us to fall into the trap of assuming that God has our shortcomings. We humans lie. Therefore, God must lie. We humans break promises. Therefore, God must break promises. How myopic of us! How blasphemous!

Encouraged by secular humanism, we grow to be more self centered and insensitive to our neighbor's needs. We betray and abandon those whom we have sworn to love. Swimming in the deceptive euphoria that humanism fosters, feeling exalted, we try to mold God in the selfsame image of the fallible and untrustworthy. When we look at the state of relationships—filial, marital, familial, and other such associations that demand trust—we should be mortified by the desertion of friends by friends and family members by family members. The suspicion or knowledge that we have been deserted by someone whom we love and trust normally brings a suffocating feeling of isolation, a morbid sense of loneliness even amidst a multitude of people. Feelings of loneliness are often amplified into hopelessness and despair, which may result even in suicide, murder-suicide, or mass murder—unless we have accepted Christ and have turned to Him for Salvation.

Suspicion that God—the Holy Trinity—Is untrustworthy corrodes our capacity for true Faith. God has good reason to be disappointed and angry with us:

> People accuse Me, without cessation, of forsaking them, just as they allege that I forsook My begotten Son when He hung on the Cross. They do not believe in the Promises that I make, even after all the Miracles that I bestow upon them. If people, who are by nature prone to sin, actually fulfill some of their promises, for instance by providing their children with food and meat, not stones, snakes, and scorpions, why do they accuse Me of breaking My Word?

As things stand in the courts of mankind—the churches, temples, mosques, and synagogues—before priests, bishops, popes, rabbis, mullahs, royalty, attendants, laypeople, and paupers—God has been arraigned and convicted by sinful men and women, who have found Him guilty of gross perjury and prevarication. Painfully enough, those who have been trained as witnesses to testify on God's behalf—to spread the Gospel to all nations, telling them what they have seen and heard—unapologetically have swung to the camp of the prosecutor. And in the full glare of all the earth, Adonai has been forsaken by His children who have willingly hearkened to the unsound counsel "If you can't beat or convert them, join them."

After we experience betrayal, paranoia impregnates doubt and births the dread of being forsaken. Suspicion gnaws at faith, and gradually replaces trust. Betrayed and forsaken by the ones that once loved and were loved, the victims drift away under the powerful influence of the current of their past negative experiences. Our human relationships suffer, and our relationship with God suffers. Suspicion replaces trust. "No, we do not want to be fooled or hurt, abandoned or forsaken again." We encase ourselves in hard-to-reach crevices of our minds, feeling secure because "no one can reach us, not even God." Thus we shrink ourselves and hide ourselves, even though King David assured us that there is no place we can hide where God will not reach us, even if we make our abode in hell. All we need do is call on Him as He has encouraged: "Call on me in times of trouble, and I will rescue you" (Psalm 50:15).

Have not even born-again and once-spirit-filled believers drifted off course because we have felt that someone in the church, an official or ordinary congregant, has broken trust with us or, worse, that God Himself has forsaken us? Such feelings may develop especially when we believers are suffering unsavory experiences such as profound losses or dreams or visions that have as yet produced no expected harvests. It is generally believed that bad things happen because God does not answer prayers or intervene on behalf of the believer. In our quandary, clutching desperately to a wobbly faith, we acquiesce with the proposition that Adonai in anger is steering us towards destruction.

Another reason why we feel betrayed and forsaken by God is that we see this relationship with God more like a social contract of convenience, one that lasts for as long as the genies respond to Aladdin's invocations and instructions. We feel betrayed and abandoned by God when "bad things happen to good people." The ridiculous thing about this self-righteous maxim is that we have judged ourselves to be "good people." "Only God is good," said Yeshua Messiah (Luke 18:19), and we would add, "all the time."

When Good Things Happen to Bad People

As believers in and followers of the Son of God, we should humbly reverse that aphorism "When bad things happen to good people" to read "When good things happen to bad people." For "bad people" is what we are. We would remain bad people, too, were it not for the Everlasting Mercy and Grace of our Eternally Loving God. God's Grace Abounds even as sin multiplies. It can withstand the wrath of Satan, whose flesh we have put on. From God's hands most of us have consciously or inadvertently received many Blessings.

Were it not for the Mercy and Loving Kindness of our Faithful God, who among us could have stood between the proverbial and literal might of Egypt and the children of Israel? Without the Shield and Shadow of the Almighty One, who would be able to tame Satan, in whose temple many of us have cavorted and sacrificed, and with whose priests and priestesses many of us have prostituted ourselves? Adonai, Who can Do Anything, Who Never Fails us.

It is hard to fully comprehend why, in spite of our innumerable and unrelenting shortcomings, our Heavenly Father has never stopped inviting us to repent, to reason together with Him, to come home like the prodigal son, to confess our sins, and to be Forgiven and Restored to Him. Yet we, in our myopia, persist in accusing Him of speaking tongue in cheek, bold-facedly lying to us, betraying our trust, abandoning us. How pathetic we allow ourselves to be?

What in the world has clouded our vision so profoundly that we see God as a prevaricator? How and where did we, in our imperfection, find the gall, the impertinence, the pernicious arrogance to make ourselves the arresting officer, prosecuting attorney, judge, and jury and to find guilty the Very One Who Is Perfection Itself? How ridiculous to act as if we fledgling students are superior in knowledge and wisdom to the One Who Is the Essence of Wisdom. A traditional African proverb asks, "Why have we tried to prove that a son begat a son before his father?" In a great travesty, *wise* has been excised from *wisdom*, and all that is left in us is *dumb* or *doom*. Thinking that we are wise, we have become fools—Satan's sitting ducks.

Our Stubbornness and Impatience

It is unsettling to recount these misrepresentations and accusations that have been advanced for over two thousand years about our Heavenly Father, the Creator of all things. Good things. We persist in the misguided thinking that, just as we are fallible, so is God, and just as we are limited in our power and knowledge, so is God. We guess at the future, collide with failed forecasts and prognostications, and constantly make adjustments to accommodate unexpected turns of events. In our ignorance and insecurity, we fault God, thinking, if He really exists, then certainly He is not actually Omniscient. Like ourselves, we insist, He can be caught unawares by events. We even accuse the Almighty of abandoning His Venerable Son, Jesus, at Calvary, by allowing His shameful death on the Cross. We prove to ourselves that God equivocates and forsakes His children, prove to ourselves that even Adonai cannot be trusted. Where in the world do we of corrupt flesh find the belly to point our accusatory finger at God and call Him a traitorous equivocator? How can we possibly challenge the very Core of His Being? And yet we persist!

Some accusations are implicit while others are explicit. The common accusation challenging All That God Is can be one or both, depending on our individual sensitivity to spiritual matters. A good example of a covert accusation surfaces in prayers such as this one: "O God, you said in your Word that whatever we ask for, through your son, will be given to us." Granted, a fearful mother might begin a prayer with just those words, her voice carrying no tone of accusation, and then say, "Please, if it is Your will, enable my daughter to recover from this terrible illness." Her prayer carries no implied or explicit accusations. But all too often, we may imply in our tone that we have every right to expect God, not only to answer our prayer, but to answer it immediately. Our microwave faith demands a microwave response: "Right now, Lord, because you said that whatever I ask you through your Son will certainly be granted to me." The Lord did not say "right now." But in our stubbornness and impatience, we demand instant gratification, just as many senders of text messages these days expect an immediate reply. After a few impatient minutes they send another text: "Didn't you get my text?"

God's Responses to our prayers and needs are rarely instantaneous, rarely like frozen dinners popped into the microwave and heated to steamy "perfection" in 6 minutes flat. God Responds to us when the time is right for us. He may, for example, Infuse our spirit with Inspiration, so that we become able to muster the thoughtfulness, courage, and fortitude to solve a particular problem that we prayed for help with. Real fixes are not usually quick fixes. Yet we are so quick to expect, not just an immediate reply, but an immediate solution. How very human of us! And then if the instant solution is not apparent, we assume God has abandoned us. There are solutions, and then there is *A Solution!*

Wholeness Through Faith

The Solution with a capital S is Faith, "which can move mountains." True Faith, wholehearted Belief in the Holy Trinity, keeps us whole, no matter what we may face in life. No matter how dreadful things may seem to us at times, true Faith assures us that God is Always With Us. We may sometimes be afraid or distraught, of course, but we know in our heart and mind and soul that He Is Seeing Us Through. Why? Because we Believe in Him and know He Is our Steadfast God. He has not forsaken us, nor will He forsake us. He will come to us right on time, His Time. God did not abandon the first sinners, Adam and Eve. Nor did He turn His back even on Cain, the first murderer. His Eye is on the sparrow, and we, the Faithful, know, as children of God, that He is watching over us. He that decorated the grass of the fields and the forest trees will always do for us Just as He Promised.

Come, my brothers and sisters, believing followers of the Path of Righteousness, let us exercise our Faith in Yeshua Messiah together. God did not abandon Adam and Eve at the very first human rebellion against His authority and instructions. It was the very first blot on the immaculate earth that He had created, the very first sin, the one that continues to birth other lower degrees of sin and rebellion such as idolatry, adultery, stealing, lying, and every other action that falls out of line with God's Commandments or Precepts. Why should He be overwhelmed, at any later time, by any other sins, no matter their quantity or quality? The only prayer that God does not answer is the one that was not prayed, and the only sin that He does not forgive is the one that was not confessed. I do not gamble, but if I had to bet, I would stake my savings and my life on the surety that Adonai will never forsake us. Let us, together, give up our stubborn impatience with Him and our stubborn misguided accusations of Him. Let us, together, embrace His Steadfast Truth.

Chapter 2

OUR MISSION TOGETHER

The Basis for the Charges

We have been exploring the persistent, unfounded charges against God in order to establish a plinth, a foundation, the causes for people's indignation and resultant indictment of the Pure One. Perhaps the root cause is people's misinterpretation of some of Christ's last words on the Cross. He spoke them in his native tongue, Aramaic: "*Eli, Eli, lama sabachthani.*" They translate into English as, "My God, My God, why have You forsaken me?" So much of our understanding and belief depends upon our grasp of intended meanings. What exactly did Jesus mean when he spoke these words? This book is based upon my study of the Bible, concordances, dictionaries, and articles and books by other theologians, as well as upon my own experiences of doubt, struggle, revelation, and belief. It uncovers and explains intended meanings of a number of key words, phrases, and sentences that are the foundation of our belief in and understanding of the Almighty, the Messiah, the Holy Spirit.

A shared understanding of such key language will increase our comprehension of God's Character and especially His

Sovereign Super-Naturalness and Omniness. Illumination will help us know enough about *the accused*, our Heavenly Father, to reject—with absolute rejection—the accusations that have been brought against Him. We will discover reasons to tremble with reverential terror whenever our wicked hearts long to further accuse Adonai of forsaking us. We will further grasp the utter foolishness inherent in a head-on collision with Him. Picture an ant scurrying along a train track smashed by a churning locomotive.

We, just like other believing followers of Jesus Messiah, sincerely desire to know God enough and sustain the wisdom and courage to tell others about His Bigness. We know that we do not know Him enough. We know that we need to know Him more. This excursion leads us on a course charted by the Holy Spirit, that we may travel past the outer courts and into the Holy Throne Room, where we may behold His Magnificence, know Him in His Infinitude, and worship Him as the Creator of All Things, whose Name is Glory Forever. Let us, together, tremble in welcome anticipation of coming Revelation.

Our Task and Key Working Terms

Together, we will serve as attorney-advocates for our one and only Client, the Mighty Infallible Godhead. In preparation for making our case to His accusers and the jury, we will, in good time, meet Him, experience Him, appreciate Him, and, to the very limited extent that we can come to understand Him Who Is Beyond Understanding, "understand" Him. To fashion our limited but essential "understanding," we will take in hand the only tools available to us. These key words generate concepts and mental images about His Wondrous, Ineffable Nature: **Omnipotent, Omniscient, Omnipresent, Immutable, Good, Just, and Worthy.** Our goal is to paint a portrait of Him Who Cannot Be Pictured but who can and does Fill our souls and who welcomes being met, experienced, appreciated, and "understood" there. The better we come to know, love, and accept Him, the better prepared we will become to make our case: to present our best portrait of Him, to weigh the accusations against Him, and to persuade His accusers and the Jury of His Absolute Innocence. Given the legions of opposition, our task is difficult. The Holy Spirit will surely Guide us. Let us now, together, with steadfastness of purpose, Faith, and confidence, embark on the cold, troubled, cleansing waters of the River Jordan.

Omnipotent

The word *Omnipotent* means, not only Almighty, which is to say, All-Powerful, but also Enormous, Huge, Gigantic, Immense, Colossal, Massive, Loud, and Deafening to degrees light years beyond our capacity to imagine. I am persuaded that, "Mathematically, all the formulae that modern and ancient cultures have used to express the immeasurably huge form but a microcosm of the Almightiness of God" (*The Vow*, 2003). Hence, for lack of adequate terminology, He can be described only inadequately as Enormously, Gigantically, Massively, Colossally Huge. Is anything, can anything be, bigger than God's Big? He can collect the waters of the earth in the Scoop of His Palm and, in the other, Hold the entirety of the universe—all that is known to us and all that is not known.

Gospel singer Kathie Lee Gifford, paying a fitting homage, offers a glimpse into God's Unknowable Power. On her album *Gentle Grace* is a song titled "He Giveth More Grace" with this chorus: "His Love has no limit, His grace has no measure, His Power has no boundaries known unto man. For out of His infinite riches in Jesus, He giveth, and giveth, and giveth again (Marantha Music, 2004; lyrics by Annie Johnson Flint and Hubert Mitchell).

Omnipotent means Supreme, Invincible, Unstoppable. As Connie, my wife articulated "All the adjectives and verbs that contemporary neologians and ancient cultures have used to express the immeasurable power or potencies of volcanic eruptions, Tsunamis, hurricanes and tornadoes, form but an insignificant fraction of the omnipotence of God" (*The Vow*, 2003).

In hopes of capturing a glimpse of God's Immense Power, let us focus on the portrait of Adonai that we are conjuring up. The Almighty God Exists Outside Space and Time, yet He Contains and Controls both. His Incomprehensible Stature and Position are Incomparable. He Bestrides Infinity like an Eternal Colossus. Yes, He does! Yet He is not *like* anything!

His Infinitude is a Mystery of the First Order, baffling philosophers, theologians, theosophists, lamas, gurus, rabbis, and masters of mysticism and metaphysics.

Our perception and conception of Infinitude, our meager attempts to encapsulate the Essences of God, fall woefully short. We are unable to grasp even the meanings of our names for Adonai. If anyone could understand God, that understanding would humble, awe, and threaten the very existence of the most powerful of monarchs. The same revelation would exalt the hope and faith of the lowest and most distraught of peasants.

Some have attempted to describe the Power of God as *Euonymus*, a Greek word from which we derive the word *Dynamite*. Theirs are noble efforts. But if we understood just a trickle of the Quality and Magnitude of the Character of Omnipotent God, we would prostrate ourselves before the Throne of Grace, repenting our sin of trivializing His Unparalleled, Incomprehensible, Infinite Disposition. Many wonder how "someone" who possesses such power, surely envied by megalomaniacs, can be so Tender and Compassionate. An African proverb presents Adonai as a metal hand holding an egg, Strong enough to protect it, equally Tender not to crush it. That is our God—and Much More than we can ever know.

If we could really look at the whole picture correctly, which of course we cannot, we would find, all evidence considered, that God is not only Powerful or All Powerful.

These adjectives describe potential human qualities. God Is the Source, the Essence, the Emanation of Power. God *Is* Power. As the sun, on a much smaller scale, is the essence of heat and light, so God *Is* Power as well as *the* Emanator of Power.

A. W. Tozer often reminds us that God's Omniness is Indefinable and Impenetrable by the common mind:

> To think rightly of God, we must conceive of Him as being altogether boundless in His goodness, mercy, love, grace and whatever else we may properly attribute to the deity. Since God is infinite, whatever He is is infinite also; that is, it must be without actual or conceivable limit. The moment we allow ourselves to think of God as having limits, the one of whom we are thinking is not God but someone or something less than and different from Him.

Omniscient

We do not need science or knowledge of Latin, Greek, or any other ancient or modern language to decipher that *Omniscient* means "All Knowing." It is a common word. When we say it, we know it means Hugeness of Knowledge. But we are incapable of imagining anything close to the concept of Knowing Everything. After all, most professionals who study the human brain, intelligence, and cognitive behavior agree that even the most adept among us actuate only 6–10 percent of our immense potential. Some have speculated that if we did use all of our potential faculties, we could know all things. Doubtful!

The very intelligent and intellectually curious Thomas Jefferson is known to have read a great many of the books available in his time on philosophy, the arts, religion, history, and science. He is known to have read English, Greek, Latin, French, Italian, Spanish, and some Anglo-Saxon (Old English). He is known to have observed the world around him astutely and to have kept meticulous notes on such things as the weather and the conditions under which certain vegetables thrived in the garden. He is known to have sent Lewis and Clark on their now-famous expedition to explore the West and find the alleged Northwest Passage to the Pacific Ocean, to keep detailed journals regarding climate, geography, navigable rivers, native peoples, plants, trees, and animals, and to bring back specimens. He is known to have attempted, as best he could, to learn all there was to know. Yet, exceptional as he was in acquiring such a wide range of knowledge for his time, what he knew was but a single stitch on the Cosmic Quilt that is God's Infinite Knowledge. Even with the descriptor "Cosmic," the word "Quilt" limits God's Knowledge to four borders, when in reality His Knowledge is Boundless.

To Know All Things, we would have to be Ubiquitous, Existing Outside Space and Time. Obviously, we are limited to the physical, three-dimensional planet earth—except for occasional ventures by a few astronauts into what we call "outer" space, which is actually not very "outer" at all. In our search for Omniscience, what we have become is ridiculous, not Ubiquitous. Our claim of human omniness is but a flight of our oversized, misguided, egocentric imagination. Our dangerous, foolish quest is born of our feverish, vaulting ambition to deify ourselves and humanize God. Scientists and students of the paranormal have been trying to fast forward into the future with successes that are actualized only in Hollywood's Halloween studios. What fools we mortals be!

It is possible that, upon reading this section on Adonai's Omniscience, some readers may project our denial of mankind's omniness onto Adonai, concluding that we have been wrong in assuming His "All-Knowingness." Such assumed deficiency in Adonai can subsequently lead to a devastating misinterpretation of the dialogue between the Father and the Son—Adonai and His Messiah, Yeshua—at the Crucifixion. What does Jesus' statement from the Cross really mean when He said, *"My Lord, my Lord, why has thou forsaken me"*? Did Adonai really forsake Christ for the reason that, alas, has been widely accepted around the Christian world? Did Jehovah really forsake Jesus because Jesus had taken unto Himself the sins of the world, thus making Himself despicable to God and worthy only of being abandoned? This question goes to the very heart of the book, and we will explore it thoroughly.

Surely God Foreknew that the first man and woman, Adam and Eve, would fall short and rebel against His

Commands. Preemptively, He offered Propitiation for the sin that they would commit. Why, then, would the Omniscient Father be surprised or repulsed when His Word came to pass at Calvary? Why would He turn His back on His Son? Why would He break His Promise never to forsake us or abandon any of us? Why, when He Foreknows each and every event in the future, would the Almighty become an equivocator?

Omnipresent

Jehovah's Omnipotence and Omniscience go hand in hand with His Omnipresence. In order to be All Powerful and All Knowing, He necessarily must be Present Everywhere All At Once: Ubiquitous, All Pervading, Universal, Ever Present. Said King David, "If I go up to the heavens, you are there; if I make my bed in the depths, you are there. If I rise on the wings of the dawn, if I settle on the far side of the sea, even there your hand will guide me, your right hand will hold me fast" (Psalm 139-8-10). (See "Appendices" for "Is God Present in Hell?")

Imagine how many crimes and other misdeeds, even the dark forces leading to misdeeds, might have been forestalled if the would-be perpetrators had been mindful of God's Abiding Presence, His Ubiquity, right there on the street corner or right there in the convenience store, Seeing All. What pedophile would lure a child into his van if he were mindful that a squad of *Navy Seals* watches over each and every child 24/7? Research shows that many misdeeds are committed behind closed doors because, somehow, perpetrators, such as adulterers, feel themselves screened from all eyes and thus safe. How misguided! Adonai is Present in every "private" office, warehouse, yacht, and back room, not only Witnessing All, but also Knowing our every thought and feeling even before it precipitates an action or reaction.

In actuality, do we not deceive ourselves even by using these familiar images to help us understand God's Universal Presence? For example, when we say that God is Forever Present in every convenience store, how many of us form in our minds a mental picture of a person or a security camera watching what goes on there? Given our human limitations, it is simply impossible for us to imagine Adonai's Everywhereness. Perhaps it will help somewhat if we say not only that He is Everywhere but also that He Is Everywhereness.

In a convenience store, on a shelf, sits a bag of coffee beans. If we open the bag and pour a handful of beans into our palm, what are we holding? If we pour all the beans into the grinding machine, select "extra fine," position the empty bag to catch the ground coffee, and push the "start" button, what flows into the bag? If we take the ground coffee to a nearby university chemistry lab and ask our chemist friend to determine the chemical make-up of a coffee granule, and he spends however long it takes to determine those chemical components, what is he finding? He discovers at least 1,000 compounds in the makeup of coffee! What is a compound? What is each compound made of? In order for him to go much deeper in his investigation, he probably has to call in his wife, who is a particle physicist. For atoms are made up of several types of smaller particles such as leptons, and there are six types of lepton: electron, electron neutrino, muon, muon neutrino, tau, and tau neutrino (Wikipedia). What on earth is a muon? It is defined as "an elementary particle similar to the electron, with unitary negative electric charge (-1) and a spin of ½." A muon "is not believed to have any sub-structure (I.e., is not thought to be composed of any simpler particles)" Wikipedia).

We are truly impressed, are we not, at how much God has enabled present-day chemists, physicists, and other scientists to learn about things, even sub-atomic things. But the definition of muon is a very telling example, is it not, of the limits of science as against the boundless, unknowable wonders and mysteries of matter and of life in Jehovah's great creation. A muon "is *not believed to have* a sub-structure" (italics mine). Sure, perhaps someday the aforementioned particle physicist will become a Nobel laureate by discovering that indeed the muon does have a sub-structure. And in time perhaps she will describe that sub-structure. But the fact—the actuality—remains that, even so, within that teeny-tiny sub-atomic muon's not-yet-discovered sub-structure dwells Adonai, who Is the Essence of All Things, including coffee and its components of more than 1,000 compounds, their atoms, their particles, and, if any, their sub-particles. More precisely and truthfully, God is the Essence, Sub-Structure, and Structure of coffee as He is of All Things living and dead, past, present, and future in the universe. That is way more

Omnipresence than we can begin to fathom! Praise the Lord for endowing us with the capacity to Believe in things we cannot begin to prove or grasp!

Immutable

A key principle in our portrait of God is that, in addition to His Omniness of Might, Knowledge, and Presence, God is Unchanging, Steadfast, Immutable. The Immutability of His Word requires neither proof nor advocacy by our personal testimonies or by twenty-first-century science and theology. We either Believe or we do not. We have the freedom to choose for ourselves and to pray that all people will choose to seek His Wisdom, the whole Truth, *the* Word.

The twentieth-century prophet A. W. Tozer (who never called himself that, unlike many of his contemporaries and ours) articulated a godly response to misguided humanistic perspectives, emphasizing, as a rock-solid foundation for Faith, the steadfastness of God's Word: "Grant me God Himself, and I am not worried about His writing a book. Grant me the being and presence of God, and that settles it." He continues, "Whenever I find men running to science to find support for the Bible, I know they are rationalists and not true believers" (G. B. Smith *Renewed Day by Day*).

Science, one of God's many provisions for us, aids us in understanding and tending His creation as best we can. But He did not intend for science to explain Him, nor could or should it, ever, for He Is Wondrously and Mysteriously Inexplicable. All we do should be done for His Glory. While scientists have discovered clues to our understanding of our planet, let not this provision cause us to switch our allegiance from God to things discovered or made by mankind. Such would be animistic, idolatrous, pagan, and self-destructive. In pure Faith lies Forgiveness, Salvation, and Eternal Life.

Tozer's powerful statement above, although inadequate, as all human statements about the Nature of God are inadequate, well represents the Creator God we seek to know, not the god that we have created, not the god that would forsake or abandon us after promising that He would not. Meditating deeply on this vital issue of Steadfastness, we transcend speculation and produce a revelation: this personality, this flip-flopping man-made god, is not the Father of our Lord and Savior, not Jehovah the Almighty. Indeed. For God the Omniscient, the Omnipotent, the Omnipresent, is also Totally Immutable. He is the Unchanging Essence and Source and Presence of All Things known and not known. Hence on what feasible grounds have some of us, His children, charged Him with breaking His Word and forsaking us?

One of the first lessons we are taught about God is that He is Infallible, His Word is Immutable, He is an Everlasting Promise Keeper, and, when He says something, He Means it, follows through on His Word, and fulfills it. He does not have to say anything more than once for us to count it as Immutable and Trustworthy. Thus, if in the entire Holy

Scriptures we read just once about God's Promise not to forsake us, we do not need anyone, high or low, king or prince, prophet, priest, pastor, laity, even angel, to give credence or value to His Word. Innumerable times He has spoken His Promise not to forsake the righteous, spoken through prophets and saints, rulers and the ruled, making clear that He will never forsake a Commandment-keeping, believing follower of His Son, the Living Christ.

Good and Just

In addition to being Omnipotent, Omniscient, Omnipresent, and Immutable, Adonai is Good and Just. His Essential Nature is Goodness, from which emanates Divine Love, Generosity, Fairness, and Mercy—Always—because He is Immutable.

He created Adam and Eve and provided a perfect habitat, the Garden of Eden. He said, "Of every tree of the garden you may freely eat" (Genesis 2:16). In them He instilled both innocence and the capacity to learn whatever they desired to learn and develop whatever they desired to develop, including language. "And God blessed them, and God said to them, Be fruitful, and multiply, and replenish the earth, and subdue it: and have dominion over the fish of the sea, and over the fowl of the air, and over every living thing that moves upon the earth" (Genesis 1:28). He entrusted Adam to name all things. He granted them freedom to make their own decisions. So that they might choose to retain their innocence, free of sin or shame, and choose to acquire only knowledge within their capacity to learn, He forbade them to eat from the Tree of Knowledge of Good and Evil. "But of the tree of the knowledge of good and evil, you shall not eat of it: for in the day that you eat thereof you shall surely die" (Genesis 2: 17).

When we think about those two vast concepts, Good and evil, which we often equate, metaphorically and literally, with Light and darkness, we realize that they represent all there is to know and understand of the universe of universes. We can't imagine even the scope of such Vast Knowledge, much less acquire the content of such Vast Knowledge. Because He is Omniscient, Jehovah Foreknew the dangers to Adam and Eve's Perfect Existence, Foreknew their choice to learn what they lacked the capacity to know.

Their decision to eat of the fruit embodied layers of self-corruption and consequences. In failing to trust and follow their Creator's Sage Command, they fell from a Perfect Life in His Grace, symbolized by Eden, into a corrupt life, symbolized by the snake that tempted Eve, Eve's subsequent temptation of Adam, a harsher environment outside the Garden, shame at their nakedness, need to clothe themselves for modesty and protection from the elements, the pain Eve had to suffer in giving birth to Cain and Abel, and Cain's murder of his brother.

The story of the Fall of Adam and Eve helps enable us, as believers or potential believers, to understand the Nature of God's Abiding Love and Fairness. He gave them just one

Commandment and the consequences for breaking it, both stated very clearly: "But of the tree of the knowledge of good and evil, you shall not eat of it: for in the day that you eat thereof you shall surely die." God's Love for them and His Generosity to them were hugely abundant, just as King David declared: "Jehovah is merciful and gracious, Slow to anger, and abundant in loving kindness" (Psalm 103:8).

Regarding God's Fairness, it is true that Eve was innocent of sin and therefore, by nature, vulnerable to temptation by the crafty, lying serpent: "'You will not certainly die,' the serpent said to the woman. 'For God knows that when you eat from it your eyes will be opened, and you will be like God, knowing good and evil'" (Genesis 3:4-5). At the same time, given Eve's innocence of sin and the clarity of His commandment, God had every reason, except His Foreknowledge of her Fall, to believe her capable of choosing to follow His Commandment despite the serpent's temptation. It is Fair and Just, is it not, for God— or for any parent—consistently to administer pre-established consequences for a clear breach of trust. God's declaration "in the day that you eat thereof you shall surely die" means, not instant physical death, but rather instant separation from God, death of innocence, knowledge of sin, certainty of eventual physical death, and damnation of the soul—were it not for His Gracious Propitiation: Merciful potential Salvation of each and every one of us through the Sacrifice of the Messiah—if we confess our sins and open our dark hearts to His Eternal Light.

Worthy

It should go without saying, then, that Adonai, who is Eternally Omnipotent, Omniscient, Omnipresent, Immutable, Good, and Just, is indeed Worthy of our absolute Faith, adoration, and gratitude. He is the Galaxies, the Planets, the Suns, the Moons, the Stars, the Sky, the Air, the Wind. He is All that we see, touch, hear, breathe, smell, taste, and imagine. He is the Sea, the Lake, the River, the Stream, the Shore, the Coastal Plain, the Dense Forest, the Jungle, the Mountain, the Valley, the High Plain. He is the Blood that flows within us. He is Paradise. Let us worship Adonai, who is at once the Father, the Son, and the Holy Spirit! Let us follow His Just Commands! Let us cherish Him always in our hearts and souls!

We Must Think Like God

However facetious, even blasphemous, it may sound for us to try to understand this concept of God's Omniness and Grace, we must open ourselves to becoming "like" God. We know that certain degrees of compatibility and reciprocity are required in every relationship that is designed to thrive and last. The Bible says we are "made in God's image." We must recapture as much of that "God's imageness" as we can, evoking the "likeness" that makes us "a chip off the Timeless Block." Although that "image" or "likeness" will radiate from our speech and mannerisms, it is, of course, not physical. Rather, it is a sparkling gem of values, beliefs, and attitudes. That gem will lead us to a greater, if inadequate, understanding of the Almighty, His creation, His Will. It will lead us to a resolute obedience to His Will. It will lead us to a reciprocity of Divine Love—Agape Love. "Birds of a feather flock together." "Tell me with whom you are friends, and I will tell you what you are." At the same time, we know that, neither literally nor figuratively, can a cow be yoked to a calf or a lion be yoked to a cub—until the Venerable Christ returns on the Great Day of Reckoning.

In order to understand something of Adonai's Omniness and obey His Commandments, "we must die to self" and assume the "likeness" in which we were originally made. For a model, we look to the Messiah, who walked as a man on the earth and yet was Always Eternally God. Upon our remaking, we will radiate the Sweet-Smelling Bouquet of Adonai, the Divine Fragrance that makes us "like" Him and attractive to Him. Underneath the soot, sweat, and gore of even a murderous criminal lives this Essence of God, poised to bring us Revelation when we allow ourselves to undergo Immersion in the Blood of the Lamb. After this Holy Cleansing, my brethren, let us endeavor to keep our vision clear. Let us avoid the fire, smoke, and soot of Satan's kitchen. Let us always resist his diabolical efforts to poison our bodies, hearts, minds, and souls. Let us always welcome and nurture our abiding kinship with Him Who Fills us with His Glorious, Omnipotent Spirit!

Emeka Anonyuo, Ph.D.

Spiritualism and Faith

Let us travel by faith and not by sight. Let us not resort to empiricism to "prove" spiritualism. We believe what we believe, do we not, because God in all His Worthiness has ordained it, not because an ancient philosopher or 21st-century scientist has proclaimed it so. Of course, empiricism has a useful place in our lives. Basically, the word denotes the belief in and practice of proving claims with information that is directly observable with our five senses aided by telescopes, microscopes, and other scientific devices. Biologists used to assume that a black bear "sleeps" all winter, hibernating in its den. To learn what a bear actually does, a contemporary biologist places a video camera in the den and actually watches the bear. For learning facts about God's physical Creation, empiricism is useful to us. Our relationship with God, however, which lives in the realm of Spirit, is quite different. It cannot be proven by empiricism, nor should we even desire it so. God is Worthy. With Him, all things are possible. We simply Believe! God endowed us with rational minds and powers of observation. We employ empiricism in preparing our gardens and growing our food. But we live by Faith in Him!

Faith is trust. We have every reason to trust the Father. We know He is Worthy. We are committed to trusting Him. But do we really trust Him? Is our Faith truly steadfast? As we live our lives, we are also committed to trusting fellow humans whom we sense to be trustworthy. Our ability to sense trustworthiness in others is much improved by our allowing ourselves to be "like" God. At the same time, we know that some among us are deliberately deceitful or "innocently" deceitful because they have been duped by someone whom they believe to be right, just as Eve believed the serpent. We do not allow ourselves to trust them. Brethren, do we allow ourselves unconsciously to project onto God the lack of trustworthiness that we too often see in our fellow humans? The quality, scope, and direction of our spiritual lives depend, do they not, on our Faith in God, on our commitment to follow His Teachings and Commandments, and, when we fail, on our willingness to humble ourselves and honestly seek His Forgiveness. Our trust, our Faith, must be rock solid. It must be so tenacious that we follow His Commandments without question or doubt. In the military, troops are expected to obey commands or else. Mere fallible humans issue those commands. How can we possibly say we are followers of God if we don't obey Him with absolute belief and trust? Our Divine God, who is Omnipotent, Omniscient, Omnipresent, Immutable, Good, Just, and Worthy asks us to live our lives within the reasonable parameters He establishes for us. Should we not view our total acceptance of Him and of His Word as a Veritable No-Brainer?

If we believe in Adonai and trust Him completely, we should believe all of His Word. "So if Adonai declared that Jonah was swallowed by a whale," said A. W. Tozer, "then, that's what happened." We do not need to fool around measuring the size of a whale's collarbone or proving how long a man can survive in a whale's stomach. Empiricism and rational thought cannot decipher God. We cannot prove God the Unfathomable by any means, even theology. Nor should we desire to try. But if we must try, it is by Faith alone that we may catch a fleeting glimpse of God's Nature, perhaps something of His Attributes, something of His Essential Being. We hear and do not see Him. We believe Him and in Him, by Faith, through Christ Jesus and the Ministry of the Holy Spirit. That is all, and It Is Everything. "Grant me God, and miracles take care of themselves," said Tozer, and we concur, do we not! Give us the key to the bank vault and the money is ours, all of it!

When Rationalists Try to Present God

When rationalists do try to present God, they make excuses as to why it is difficult to understand Him. They apply logic and apologetics to try and simplify the Mystery of Divinity and make it comprehensible. By the time empiricism exhausts its theories, Adonai is so simplified and humanized that the measly portrait likely repels true believers. We know by Faith that God the Omnipotent is So Much Greater in Divine Attributes than the beggarly "being" depicted as embodying qualities no greater than those of an ordinary mortal. So we find the statement worthy of study that "God made man in His image and likeness, and man returns the favor by casting God in man's image and likeness" (Vow 2003). Alas, this man-made god, emasculated of Divinity, becomes an errand boy to his human maker, a mere Saint Nicholas or Father Christmas or Ali Baba, with his secret access code, "Open sesame."

By and large, depictions of God in science, legend, and mythology belittle Him. In science, He is either nonexistent or works in conjunction with natural forces, and in legend and mythology, He is but a glorified man—often a facsimile of the ancient Greek and Roman gods and goddesses. His status is set by humans and can be adjusted to suit our quirks. Sometimes, He is seen as a chore boy, the genie out of Aladdin's lamp who satisfies our wishes and fantasies. If He "fails" to satisfy our individual and collective expectations and indulgences, He is indicted and found guilty of forsaking and breaking His Covenant—not fulfilling His Promises. What should gladden the hearts of true believer-followers of Christ is the fact that, no matter what we think, say, believe, or do, Almighty God Remains Almighty God.

Anticipating the Trial

Given the unquestionable Omniness of Adonai, we travel forward with confidence to defend Him. As attorneys for the defense of the Almighty Jehovah, we will allow the prosecuting attorneys, the inquisitors, to make their case.

In medieval Europe the Roman Catholic Church launched a movement to prosecute and punish virtually everyone whose beliefs or practices deviated from official church doctrine. The perpetrators were said to be *heretics*, their crime was said to be *heresy*, and the movement came to be known as the *Inquisition*. Here, the attorneys for the prosecution, consisting of misguided, disgruntled unbelievers or misbelievers worldwide, charge God Himself with the crime of having forsaken Jesus on the Cross and, likewise, of forsaking us, God's children, by going back on His word. The word *forsake* means to abandon, renounce, relinquish, turn your back on, desert, leave, disown. Does Adonai ever do this; equivocate?

It seems ironic for misguided, disgruntled unbelievers and misbelievers to renounce the Truth of God's Holy Word and dare to charge our perfect Lord with the crime of heresy. They allege that He broke His Word to Jesus and His Word to us. Satan works in odious ways! Our job as attorneys for the defense is to hear the charges tolerantly, weigh them, and counter them with every fiber of our being. Although we know the Truth, we must prove it in open court. In this unique case, the jury is all the people of the world, faithful believers, waffling believers, unbelievers, and misbelievers. Our goal—and the heart of this book—is to reveal to the world's people that, whatever our own particular religion or beliefs, our One True God, in all His Omniness, is Infinitely Trustworthy and, therefore, Innocent of heresy.

Proving Adonai Faultless Is a Difficult Task, In the 21st Century

The inquisitors do face a difficult challenge convincing the jury that God forsook Jesus at Golgatha, has forsaken us, the righteous, and will forsake future believers. For evidence, they will cite biblical passages and offer their own subjective, slanted interpretations. Their charges will contradict what we know to be God's Eternal Trustworthiness and Consistency of Character. They will paint Jehovah as if He were psychologically unstable, a kind of mental patient estranged from Himself, incapable of the Loving Consistency that we know to be His True Essential Nature. We know God to be Always and Forever the God that we know Him to be. But now we must prove what we know. And while we represent what is Right and Good, given the abundance of waffling believers, unbelievers, and misbelievers, we, too, face a challenging task.

What Makes This Task a Challenging One?

As mere mortals, we are, of course, imperfect, given the fall of Eve and Adam from God's grace. Those of us who believe in Adonai with all our hearts and souls and who embrace the Lord Jesus Christ as our Savior—we do our best to live our lives as "perfectly" as we can, following God's Commandments. Although by nature we are sinners, we do our best to live our lives free of further sin. Human imperfection allows or even stimulates some among us to fall deeper and commit the heinous act of forsaking others, especially those who have sinned first. Instead of turning the other cheek, as Jesus so wisely advises, and forgiving others, they forsake their fellow humans. Or worse, they forsake God.

If we all were "Perfect" and thus endowed with Omniscience, we could foretell the future. We could envision, for example, that our prospective spouse, at a certain time in the future, would become unfaithful, would violate the sacred vows of marriage. As the caring potential spouse of that person, we could choose to go forward with the marriage while taking thoughtful, constructive action to improve the relationship moment to moment, perhaps thus preventing our spouse from developing the desire to seek the intimate company of another. If we did go ahead with the marriage and, despite our good-faith efforts, the infidelity did occur, we could foretell its impact on our spouse and, if seemingly justified, forgive the breach and mend the relationship. Or, as the caring prospective spouse of someone whom we foresee as capable of infidelity, we could break off the engagement and seek a spouse who, we foreknow, will remain committed to the marriage vows.

Since in reality we are not Omniscient, we can only strive to make godly choices and live our lives as best we can. Our inability to chart the course of our destiny often results in missteps and regret. As the inquisitors are fond of saying, does not God suffer from the same malady, inability to foreknow the future of missteps and regret? Even though occasionally we may find in the Holy Scriptures statements *seeming* to suggest that God repented or regretted His action, we should read more carefully, never allowing ourselves the misguided thought that Adonai has ever fallen short or ever will fall short in His Eternal Constancy or in any Dimension of His Being. Such destructive thoughts may pervade our minds, especially as we struggle to understand and cope with the degree of God's displeasure with us at times, as revealed by the Lord's Word in the Holy Scriptures or by His powerful, if silent, Voice within us.

Our potential for understanding is greater than the adequacy of our vocabulary, which helps us understand, yes, but at the same time prevents our understanding of That

Which Is Beyond Knowing. The Silent Voice of Adonai, the Gracious One, offers us Wisdom that cannot be accessed otherwise and that cannot be received or explained in words. His Tutelage via the Holy Spirit reveals, to us of Faith, the Unseen, Unspoken Truth: the Almighty is Purity Itself, utterly free of fault, and thus has nothing to regret or apologize for. "God is not a man, that he should lie; neither the son of man, that he should repent" (Numbers 23:19). His every action has always proceeded and always will proceed from His Perfect Essence, including his Plan for and Creation of the Universe.

As Trish, my friend's six-year-old daughter, convalesced after having been attacked by her puppy, she lamented that if she had known her puppy Digger was going to be such a "jerk," she would have taken her pup's sister instead. Trish's lament was over her inability to foreknow the future. God does not suffer this deficiency. He Created and Knew All Things before they became reality, much as human architects envision the completed building before completing their plans. How much more Visionary the Supreme Architect God!

Adonai Sustains all things, Can Do all things, Can Undo all things. In a poem, the inspired 19th-century poet Emily Dickinson declared, "The bird does not resume the egg." True, we humans cannot turn back time. Once events have taken place, we cannot undo them. But our Father God, if He so desires, can hold in His palm a newly hatched bluebird, re-constitute the broken shell, return the bird to its pre-hatched state, and re-place the egg inside the mother bird. With Him, All Things Are Possible, whether known or unknown. When He said, "Earth be," from nothing the earth appeared. God is not little Trish, who would have done things differently if she had had the ability to foretell events in the future. We lack adequate words to describe His Capabilities. When we say, "Adonai Knows the future," we know the words and their worldly meanings, but we grasp little of the Nature and Scope of His Hugeness Beyond Knowing. For God, past, present, and future are one. How is such possible? We have no idea, although we know the words mean that He Sees Them at One Time All Together. Brethren, that is why He is *El Shaddai* and we are not. However, that we, in fact, can fathom very little, all things considered, should not ever birth doubt in our minds and hearts and souls as to the Existence and Rightness of His Truth.

The Accusation

Even to think such a misguided, frightening thought would be bad enough. To declare aloud that God forsook His Son would be blasphemy, heresy, tantamount to calling Adonai a liar and a traitor. Yet, for over two thousand years, He has been so accused, mostly by the very Christians who claim to be His. The accusation is utterly preposterous that God forsook His Son on Calvary because Jesus was no longer worthy to be His Son. In reality, Jesus was fulfilling His Divine Destiny to take unto Himself all of the world's sins heaped together and to suffer a horrific death so that those of us who repent might be Forgiven of all sin and Granted Eternal Life in Heaven. In the misguided view of the inquisitors, Jesus, as though a mere man, had allowed Himself to become corrupted by the sins of the world, thus rendering Himself unworthy in God's eyes.

This ludicrous claim implies that God the Father and God the Son are not One. It implies that God is not Omniscient but flawed, incapable of Foreknowing Christ's physical and mental condition on the Cross as the Bearer of the world's sins. Were the claim true, it would imply that God, as if an ordinary person, can be taken unawares, not only by events but by His own emotions. In truth, El Shaddai is Superhuman, greater than Alpha and Omega. Never slumbering, He remains Perfectly Mindful of His creation, Watching, Protecting, Providing. Those who believe in Him answer His Call, keep His Commands, worship and adore Him. Even the rebellious inquisitors are in His thoughts. He shelters even them with His Grace. His rain falls on the crops of the righteous as well as on the crops of the unrighteous. Manifestation of His Mercy, Grace, and Love is Indeed Boundless!

Christ's Puzzling Words

The scriptures say that in the ninth hour on the day of His Crucifixion, our Venerable Master, Jesus the Messiah, cried out with a loud voice, *"Eloi, Eloi, lama sabachthani* [My God, my God, why have you forsaken me?] Why are You so far from helping me, and from the words of my groaning?" (Mark 15:34, Matthew 27:46; 27:35, 39, 43; and John 19:23–24, 28). King David, in the throes of his own fear and anxiety, cried out to God with the same words (Psalm 22:1). Our essential question is, Why?

Both seem to have been expressing deep anguish. As fellow humans, while we can't feel much of what David was actually going through, especially given his roles of great responsibility as a king and a prophet, perhaps we can, to some degree, imagine his suffering. In doing so, it is perhaps necessary and justifiable for us to "project" onto him and onto his experience what we understand about being human. The two thieves beside Jesus, were, in all likelihood, weighed down by regret, other emotions, their own body weight, and the terrible pain of dying slowly, hung on crosses as they were. As fellow humans, perhaps we can, to some extent, imagine their anguish as perhaps we can King David's.

But when it comes to understanding and explaining the experience of the Messiah on the Cross, we bear witness to a very different set of circumstances. Although Jesus walked the earth as if He were a man, He remained God the Divine. When discussing His Crucifixion, it is essential that we not "project" onto Him and onto His experience what we understand about being human. We may wish, but we must not allow ourselves, to assume, for example, that He suffered the same physical pain as the two thieves crucified beside him. We must not assume that, in taking upon Himself the sins of the world, He bore on his shoulders a zillion-ton cloak of lead sin. We must not assume that, in taking all that sin upon Himself, He became corrupted by it. We must not allow ourselves to assume that God the Father forsook or abandoned God the Son, even for a moment, for They and the Holy Spirit Are One Holy Divine Being. We must not assume that Christ's Ascension into Heaven was made possible by the wings of angels or, worse, by the Starship Enterprise. In other words, we must *know* in our hearts, minds, and souls that, in every moment, even of His Crucifixion, Resurrection, and Ascension, Christ remained God the Divine with All His Precious, Incomprehensible Omniness! King David remained human. Christ remained God the Divine. And yet they spoke the same words! Praise the Lord for working in Ways so Mysterious and Glorious!

Jesus walked the earth as if He were a man of flesh and blood, yes, but He was not, as many argue, part man and part God. He was Wholly God, with all the Infinite, Incomprehensible Omniscience, Omnipotence, Omnipresence, Immutability, Goodness, Fairness, and Worthiness appertaining to God. To fulfill His Divine Destiny as the Messiah, He chose to appear to us as both man and God at once. He allowed Himself to be crucified, which, of course, for an earthling inflicts a long-suffering, horrific death. As well, He chose to take upon Himself, as we say, all the sins of the world, an act that is totally beyond our comprehension—and yet an act that our Faith enables us to appreciate beyond all knowing. Given our human fallibility, let us not venture to make up rational explanations regarding our Christ's experience and suffering. Such explanations lie beyond our meager capacity. Instead, let us venture forth with Faith and gratitude for His Divine Propitiation as presented in the Holy Bible.

Perhaps it is an understandable, if misguided, assumption, made by many, that, temporarily, Jesus actually became a man and, in so doing, temporarily, ceased to be God the Divine. Such assumptions can aid us mere humans in rationalizing answers to tough questions. Sometimes we readily accept an obvious answer rather than dig for a deeper one, or, more profoundly, given the Wondrous Mystery of All Things Spiritual, we learn to accept and live joyfully with what we cannot know. A simple, misguided, answer would be that it was the man Jesus, not the Messiah Jesus, who cried out, "My God, my God, why have you forsaken Me?"

Even if the Messiah Jesus had chosen to endow Himself temporarily with the human trait of extreme sensitivity to physical pain and emotional anguish—though let us not speculate that He did so—surely, given his Self-Appointed Mission, He would have sustained His Ability to withstand even unimaginable physical pain and emotional anguish without giving in to despair—without breaking. As well, just because Christ took all the sins of the world unto Himself does not mean that He, Himself, became in any way soiled or corrupted by that sin. Likewise, His Father, our Father, who is Infinitely Sensitive and Empathetic to all beings in His Creation, is immune to such vindictive emotional reactions as the inquisitors allege.

Adonai is demanding, yes, even at times Angry with us for our errant thoughts and behavior. But He is not vindictive. Nothing breaks the Will of God. God does not break His Word. God does not forsake. God is Infinitely Trustworthy.

It was in acknowledgement of this fact that my wife and I named our second child *Onyekachi,* an *Igbo-African* name that translates to "Who is greater than God?" The name is not a question but a rhetorical question, a spirited, respectful affirmation that no one is greater or mightier than Adonai.

First David, Then Jesus Messiah

Before we further examine the words Jesus spoke on the cross, let us consider the words of King David, who uttered the very same words. When we read David's various expressions of fear, anguish, frustration, and hopelessness, we may notice apparent inconsistencies and contradictions, yes. But, if we are to reach understanding, our responsibility is not to take his "ranting" merely at face value. He wrote, "I have been young and now am old, yet I have never seen the righteous forsaken or their children begging bread" (Psalm 37:25). He also wrote, "My God, my God, why have you forsaken me?" (Psalm 22).

Being human, David lived through many contradictory experiences and reactions. It is common, given human weakness, for us to *feel* forsaken sometimes even though we have not actually been forsaken. So much of David's writing in the scriptures provides assurances that God always provides for the righteous. By crying out to God, "Why have you forsaken me?" the very wise psalmist was not blaming God at all, but rather searching for his connection with God that, at the time, seemed lost to him. David had strayed from righteousness, was feeling plagued by confusion, guilt, and anxiety, was struggling to understand, and was praying desperately to God for relief. This is quite a different way of interpreting what we initially may have sensed to be "inconsistencies and contradictions."

The following two passages from Psalm 22 reveal his complex state of mind:

> My God, my God, why have you forsaken me? Why are you so far from helping me, and from the words of my roaring? O my God, I cry in the day time, but you hear not; and in the night season, and am not silent. But you are holy, O you that inhabit the praises of Israel. Our fathers trusted in you: they trusted, and you did deliver them. They cried to you, and were delivered: they trusted in you, and were not confounded. But I am a worm, and no man; a reproach of men, and despised of the people (1-6).

> My strength is dried up like a potsherd; and my tongue sticks to my jaws; and you have brought me into the dust of death. For dogs have compassed me: the assembly of the wicked have enclosed me: they pierced my hands and my feet. I may tell all my bones: they look and stare on me. They part my garments among them, and cast lots on my clothing. But be not you far from me, O LORD: O my strength, haste you to help me. Deliver my soul

from the sword; my darling from the power of the dog. Save me from the lion's mouth: for you have heard me from the horns of the unicorns. I will declare your name to my brothers: in the middle of the congregation will I praise you (15-22).

Perhaps David was, at times, stooping to blame God for his own missteps because, having gone astray by his own failings, he was too overcome with negative emotions to take responsibility for his actions and state of mind. Still, even in the clutches of his intense anguish, choked by feelings of separation from God, David never accused God of failing to look out for all who are righteous. In fact, he exonerates God: "In all my days, I have never seen the righteous forsaken" (Psalm 37:25).

Those of us trying to live with purity of spirit may understand and appreciate King David's willingness to own up to his failures and to reiterate his unflinching Faith and Trust in *Adonai*. He wrote, "For innumerable evils have compassed me about; my iniquities have taken such hold on me that I am not able to look up. They are more than the hairs of my head, and my heart has failed me and forsaken me" (Psalm 40:12). David knew the reasons why evils were befalling him: indeed his own failures of righteousness were numerous. He admitted that he had strayed and that God delivered him by allowing him to suffer intense tribulations and trials.

The joyful lesson is that Adonai restored David to righteousness and that, if any of us—Catholic or Protestant,

Charismatic or Pentecostal, Jew or gentile, Muslim or Sikh, Hindu or Buddhist, clergy or laity—confesses our transgressions, God will Forgive and Restore us. However tenaciously Satan may tempt us not to believe this Fundamental Truth, and while we, like David, are bound to experience personal strife, our Faith remains steadfast. We know our God is the Rock of Ages. We know He Hears us, Forgives us, Loves us, and Restores us to His Keeping. Anyone who doubts or disagrees may be counted among the cohort of Satan! But you must renounce wickedness, confess your sins and willingly accept Yeshua Messiah as your Lord, and Savior; the Way, the Truth, Life, and Light of the World.

How many of us twenty-first-century Christians confess our sins so honestly as David did? The Psalms might as well be chiseled on stone tablets, for they constitute timeless touchstones, precious to anyone who desires to cultivate a true and abiding relationship with the Almighty. Honesty with oneself and with God is paramount. Just after Eve and Adam ate the forbidden fruit, they felt self-conscious, naked, and ashamed. "And they heard the sound of the Lord God walking in the garden in the cool of the day, and Adam and his wife hid themselves from the presence of the Lord God among the trees of the garden. Then the Lord God called to Adam and said to him, 'Where are you?' So he said, 'I heard Your voice in the garden, and I was afraid because I was naked; and I hid myself.' And He said, 'Who told you that you were naked? Have you eaten from the tree of which I commanded you that you should not eat?'" (Genesis 3:8-11).

Adam, to whom God had given earthly authority and responsibility, might have chosen to respond with maturity, honesty, and honor. He might have humbled himself to God, confessed that he had broken God's command, and sought God's forgiveness. What did Adam do? He blamed Eve: "The woman whom You gave to be with me, she gave me of the tree, and I ate" (Genesis 3:12). Worse, Adam also blamed God, did he not, for having given him "the woman." Likewise, when God said to Eve, "What is this you have done?" she replied, "The serpent deceived me, and I ate" (Genesis 3:13). She, too, failed to take personal responsibility and seek forgiveness. Deception by the serpent was no excuse. We cannot, of course, know how God might have responded had both Adam and Eve taken responsibility and humbly sought Absolution. Perhaps the outcome might have been quite different for God's human creatures.

Are we not, in these times, much like Adam and Eve? Do we even wince when we blame God for allowing a tree to fall on our house? Do we not intellectualize and rationalize our misdeeds? Do we not simplify and make mundane even the most potentially meaningful spiritual phenomenon? We can't begin to imagine all the mistrust and even hate that Adonai must endure, despite the steady flow of testimony to His Unrelenting Faithfulness to His whole creation. His Divine Authenticity has been declared profusely and profoundly, unequivocally and unapologetically, by King David, by many other prophets of old, and by hosts of others down through the ages. David's own words, above, here, and elsewhere, destroy the argument that God forsook him: "Although my father and my mother have forsaken me, yet the Lord will take me up and adopt me as His child" (Psalm 27:10).

Many contemporary theologians constitute an unfortunate, lethal admixture of "wisdom" from ancient pagan Greece and Rome and from postmodernist flair. Like the enemies of David, they seem confused as to what is really happening. Failing to discern the Hand of our Lord in the affairs of the world, David's adversaries made a self-destructive assumption: "God has forsaken him; pursue and persecute and overtake him, for there is none to deliver him" (Psalm 71:11). This was the misguided understanding held by the enemy, who felt that, since they were overwhelming David, his God must have deserted him. Were they right? Did God really forsake David? The enemy thought so, but they were dead wrong. David, despite his litany of woes, proclaimed the Goodness, Righteousness, and Sovereignty of Adonai. He still believed in and trusted the Lord even though God allowed him to suffer much anguish brought on by rebellion and many other worldly tribulations. King David, although a great man with much power and influence, was far from perfect. But he remained brave, thoughtful, and steadfast in proclaiming the Abiding Glory, Loyalty, and Greatness of Jehovah, unlike the fashionable skeptical "thinkers" so prevalent today.

Besides, if Adonai had actually abandoned David, why would David still have prayed to Him? The Holy Scriptures tell us that a supplicant who is unrighteous and unregenerate, who is, at heart, a reprobate, is an affront to God, just as Eve and Adam were. If Adonai had rejected or forsaken David, He would have rejected his prayers, too, and the enemy, resultantly, would have overcome him. But did they? They did not. God never abandoned David even though he may have thought so at the time. "The Name of the Lord is a strong tower, the righteous run into it, and they are saved" (Proverbs 18:10). "The Lord is my light and my salvation—whom shall I fear? The Lord is the stronghold of my life—of whom shall I be afraid?"(Psalm 27:1). "The Lord is my Shepherd, I shall not want" (Psalm 23:1). Nor did He abandon Adam and Eve!

Behold the Lamb

Jesus the Lamb—and the Shepherd—was born for one purpose: to take away the sins of the world and, by His Sacrifice, Reconcile mankind to God the Father. Yeshua's Crucifixion on the Cross was *the* Bridge between Heaven and earth, between God the Creator and His sinful, rebellious creation. We may desire to imagine all the sins of the world pressing down upon the shoulders of Jesus. For us as humans, it seems reasonable to wonder, at what point in time did that immense mass of sin gravitate to Him and at what point in time did He shed it? The middle section of the Apostle's Creed, a creed not popular around non Roman Catholics briefly summarizes Christ's experience, and may aid us in addressing such questions:

> Jesus Christ . . . was conceived by the Holy Ghost, born of the Virgin Mary, suffered under Pontius Pilate, was crucified, dead, and buried; He descended into hell; the third day He rose again from the dead; He ascended into heaven, and sits

on the right hand of God the Father Almighty;
from there He shall come to judge the living and
the dead."

Obviously, the Apostles' Creed does not include the
entombment of Jesus' body in a cave, with a boulder covering
the entrance, or the events that transpired there, from
whence He Rose from the dead and Ascended into Heaven.
The statement considered the most controversial among
theologians is, "He descended into hell." Some interpret "hell"
figuratively to signify, in a word, either Christ's suffering and
death or His letting go of all the sins of the world. Others
interpret "hell" literally to signify Jesus' entering hell actually
and leaving all the sins of the world in Satan's horrific lair.

Just as with the old theological question (or is it
geographical?) "How many angels can dance on the head of
a pin," we, as humans, will never be able to determine just
when or how or where Jesus took upon Himself and later
shed the sins of the world. Perhaps it transpired in a flash of
Holy Grace and Mercy when Christ declared, "It is finished,"
as though His time in the flesh on earth were over, the mass
of sin had left him, and he would now return to live again in
Heaven. Of course, the Messiah, while assuming the body and
blood of a mortal man, always retained and retains all of the
same qualities, such as Omniscience and Goodness, that are
Embodied by God the Father. However people may choose to
interpret "He descended into hell," the truth is that the Messiah,
having assumed the body and blood of a man, did die a cruel
death on the cross; did take unto Himself, and then eventually

shed, all the sins of the world, past, present, and future; did rise from the dead; and did ascend into Heaven to sit at the right hand of God, the Father. Let us not waste our time attempting to calculate or explain how many angels can dance on the head of a pin. Brethren, let us open our hearts and believe in and follow Christ our Lord and Savior!

When the inquisitors charge Adonai with forsaking Jesus and His flock, even if they include no direct charge against Jesus, by implication they are claiming that Jesus, in turn, forsook His Father and His flock. In their misguided, blasphemous view, when Jesus took unto Himself all the sins of the world, He allowed Himself, His essential Messiah self, to be corrupted by that mass of sin. Thus, they falsely claim, He was no longer the pure Lamb of God. No longer was He Worthy, they falsely claim, of His Father's Love and Keeping. If Christ's physical or spiritual Being had, at any time before, during, or after the Calvary ordeal, been attracted to sin, then He would have become unfit to be one of the Holy Trinity. We know the Truth, do we not, and if we subscribe to It, our Savior God will Hold us to His Loving Breast and Absolve us of our sins.

The Goodness of God and the evilness of Satan are permanently irreconcilable since they are diametrically opposite. It would be impossible for the devil to positively bless anyone because he cannot give what he does not have: Goodness, Blessedness. Likewise, it would be impossible for God to curse anyone because He cannot give what He does not have: hatefulness or evil. The devil, as far as we know, is happy and satisfied to be the master of evil and would not be flattered should anyone ascribe to him the Attributes of God. Yes, he would like to be called God but would nonetheless remain the prince of darkness. No doubt Satan would have been delighted to learn that both God the Father and Jesus the Son had forsaken one another and humanity. What must threaten the vile prince of darkness every moment of every day is the dreaded Certainty that the Holy Attributes that make God God and the Son the Son and the Holy Spirit the Holy Spirit will continue to flood the universe with Light, Hope, Love, Forgiveness, Certainty, Faith, Holiness, and Eternal Life—Always.

Between north and south and east and west, perhaps there could be some reconciliation, but between darkness and Light, evil and Good, hell and Heaven, Satan and God, there is no cease-fire. The Bible tells us that the flesh will constantly battle with the Spirit. The prince of darkness enters wherever and whatever he can. The flesh alone, empty of the Holy Spirit, is a vessel awaiting Satan's corruption. Jesus was conceived by the Holy Spirit in Mary's womb and was born into the world as a human infant of flesh and blood and yet was always filled completely by His Divine Spirit. Christ Always remained and remains Totally God.

Just as we cannot begin to imagine the Omniness of God, we cannot, for at least two reasons, begin to imagine all the sins of the world amassed. While many sins are physical actions that can be filmed or imagined, the essence of sin lives in our less-than-perfect minds, hearts, and spirits. We sin, whether in thought, word, or deed, because we choose to sin. Sure, we may like to rationalize that evil, Satan, within us causes us to sin. But, in actuality, we have within us the capacity not to sin, just as Eve had the capacity, but not the will, to resist the crafty serpent. We have experienced hundreds or thousands or millions of moments, have we not, when we have felt tempted to sin but have chosen not to commit the act, whether it be relishing an evil thought that pops into mind, lying, cheating, stealing, or slapping someone. Because of our own experience, we can, to some extent, imagine how others may choose to sin or not to sin. But considering how many sins each human commits in a lifetime, try as we may, we simply cannot begin to imagine all the sins of the world, past, present, and future.

How Much Sin Would Corrupt Adonai?

Likewise, we lack adequate language to describe or explain the Colossal, Incomprehensible Mission of Jesus in taking upon Himself all the sins of the world. We know that the flesh-and-blood man Jesus was Infused Eternally with Divine Spirit and always remained a Bastion of Purity, Incorruptible by Satan, completely without sin. He was made to lug his own brutally heavy Cross to Calvary. Although we cannot begin to imagine the unimaginable, in our desire to grasp the Suffering of Jesus, we may be tempted to picture "all the sins of the world" surrounding Him as, let us say, a vast invisible but brutally heavy "cloud." Of course, only He, the Father, and the Holy Spirit would be able to sense its heavy, dark presence, weighing upon

Emeka Anonyuo, Ph.D.

Him—but in no way entering Him or corrupting Him. While He Who Was, Is, and Always Will Be Without Sin willingly bore its unimaginably heavy burden, no darkness seeped into Him. For there was not a "cloud" at all but, rather, *Believe* and not attempt to picture the Inexplicable.

Sacrificial Beasts Were Clean, Why Should Adonai's, Yeshua Messiah, Be Said to be "Unclean", Causing Adonai to "Turn Away His Face, and Forsake His Son"

My son Tobechukwu said, "Adonai wanted someone who looked like the man and woman that Satan deceived, someone who looked like Adonai, to bring low the spirit of disobedience. He found none, so He chose Himself, and borrowed a costume of flesh, but kept His attributes, His divinity." Even the sacrificial lamb, goat, calf, or any other animal to be sacrificed for the cleansing of people in the Eyes of God had to be perfect, without blemish. That was God's requirement for Cain and Abel. Anything less was unacceptable to Him. If that is the case with beasts, would Divine Expectations of the Messiah Lamb be less? Surely not!

Cain and Abel Foreshadow Christ's Sacrifice

God gave us the story of Cain and Abel as a perfect illustration of perfect sacrifice, sacrifice totally acceptable to Him. We all know the story: Cain's blemished sacrifice failed to meet God's standard. God rejected it. Abel's willing sacrifice of unblemished animals pleased God. He accepted it. Envious of Abel's higher status in God's eyes, Cain murdered his brother.

This iconic story of acceptable sacrifice foreshadows the Supreme Sacrifice of Jesus on the Cross, although the unblemished animals that Abel willingly offered had no choice in their fate. God the Father, Son, and Holy Spirit decided together that Jesus would go down to earth to live as if He were a man and eventually atone for all the sins of the world, and Jesus gave Himself willingly. Jesus was the Perfect Lamb presented for Sacrifice, totally acceptable to God as Atonement for our vast multitude of sins. There was no forsaking in either direction.

God's dealings with the hard-hearted, stiff-necked generations of Israelites and, down through the ages, the rest of mankind demonstrate His Steadfast Constancy, Love, Mercy, and Grace. Despite the ungrateful, mean-spirited rebelliousness of "His chosen people," Adonai continues to be Inerrant, His Exalted Word being His Bond. He never changes. So as He Was in the Beginning, He Is Now and will Remain the Same Forever. Let us worship Him with adoration!

The Testimony of Isaiah

Testimony by the prophet Isaiah also confirms God's Innocence in the alleged forsaking of Christ. Anointed by God, Isaiah prophesied the coming of the Messiah, foretelling that mankind, not God, would despise and forsake Jesus: "He was despised and rejected and forsaken by men, a Man of sorrows and pains, and acquainted with grief and sickness; and like One from Whom men hide their faces He was despised, and we did not appreciate His worth or have any esteem for Him" (Isaiah 53:3). If Jehovah the Omniscient Foreknew that Christ would become corrupted by sin, Isaiah's prophecy would have read, 'He was rejected and forsaken by God, His Father, . . . and like One from whom God hides His face, He was despised, and God, His Father, did not appreciate His worth or have any esteem for Him." No, the prophet had heard clearly and directly from Adonai and penned exactly what God dictated. Let us not allow the prince of darkness to undermine our Faith and our knowing: Both the Father and the Son Were, Are, and Always Will Be the Essence of Purity, Infused with the Holy Spirit.

The Testimony of Jeremiah

Jeremiah, who, like Isaiah, was ordained by God and endowed by the Holy Spirit, also testified to the unswerving Faithfulness of God: 'For Israel has not been widowed and forsaken, nor has Judah, by his God, the Lord of hosts, though their land is full of guilt against the Holy One of Israel' (Jeremiah 51:3). This powerful statement implicitly declares, "Though your sins be blood red, I, your God, will not turn away and abandon you, but will wash you white as snow. Simply confess your guilt to Me." Brethren, Divine Forgiveness is exactly why Jesus Christ came into the world.

Nothing takes God unawares: "I knew you before I formed you in your mother's womb" (Jeremiah 1:5). Was He not Here before the beginning! Will He not Remain after the end! Alpha and Omega! First and Everlasting!

Day of Infamy, Day of Vindication

We strive to understand and tolerate the waffling believers, unbelievers, and misbelievers who challenge the Inerrancy of the Word and of God Himself. We have been analyzing the Words of our Venerable Messiah, spoken from the Cross on that day of shame and infamy. On that fateful day, we humans exceeded our prior capacity for wickedness and cruelty. We declared a Man of Spotless Innocence guilty and sentenced Him to experience a horrific death. But Glory and Honor to God our Father! His Power of Resurrection thwarted the enemy and brought forth the King of Glory! Satan, even with help from people whom the Messiah came to redeem, could not hold down His Sacred Body in the tomb. On the third day, Innocence was vindicated, Resurrected, and Enthroned in Heaven. And so shall be Resurrected all of us who welcome into our hearts the Lamb who was slain!

Was Yeshua Messiah Perplexed on the Cross?

Christ taught that He, the Father, and the Holy Spirit together were the architects of His incarnation, ministry, death and Resurrection. How, then, could He have been perplexed on the Cross? How possibly could He have felt abandoned by His Father? Every word and deed of the Messiah, literally and figuratively, testifies to the fact that He participated in the Creation of all things, willingly abdicated His Heavenly Throne, temporarily, and came to earth to be the Way, the Truth, the Light, the Life of the world. His arrest and Crucifixion were integral parts of Their Divine plan to ransom sinful mankind, therefore bringing the words of the prophets to Fulfillment. Proof of such lies in the Gospel of John. When the men came to arrest Jesus, among them were the Jewish High Priest Caiaphas and his servant: "Then Simon Peter having a sword drew it, and smote the high priest's servant, and cut off his right ear. The servant's name was Malchus. Then said Jesus unto Peter, Put up thy sword into the sheath: the cup which my Father hath given me, shall I not drink it?" (John 18:10-11; the same is also told in the Gospels of Matthew, Mark, and Luke). Clearly, Jesus Foreknew His Divine Destiny and embraced it, however horrific.

Evidence is replete in the Holy Scriptures that the Venerable Messiah, a Member of the Godhead, existed from the beginning with the Father before all things were made. The Apostle John wrote, "In the beginning was the Word, and the Word was with God, and the Word was God" (John 1:1). The oldest surviving complete Christian Bibles are Greek manuscripts from the 4th century. The Greek word logos, translated into English as "the Word," originally meant "a ground," "a plea," "an opinion," "an expectation," "word," "speech," "account," "reason" (Wikipedia). Clearly, logos was, and is, a highly charged word resonating with significance.

John also wrote, "The Word became flesh and made his dwelling among us. We have seen his glory, the glory of the One and Only, who came from the Father, full of grace and truth" (John 1:14). Without doubt, this passage identifies Jesus as "the Word." Hence the declaration "In the beginning was the Word" means, so Wondrously, so Hopefully, so Divinely, that before there was anything, there was Everything: not only the Hope of Eternal Salvation, but the Promise of Eternal Salvation. In the beginning was not Jesus , but Logos, "the Word," the Incomprehensible, the Divine, the Infinite, the Glorious Conceptualization of what was to be Forevermore. Where? In the Cosmic Mind of the Father, the Son, and the Holy Spirit. What? The Rock-Solid Promise that Salvation and Eternal Life would be made Real when the Venerable, Omniscient Jesus, the Messiah, walked the earth and was crucified as if He were a man.

Our Buddy God

As we see, understanding why Christ cried "My God, My God . . ." has been shadowed by misconceptions. What has thrown so many well-meaning people into confusion is the conception of Christ as a "shape-shifting" man-God. In their misguided view, the Son of God who is Himself God, sometimes assumes the role of a man, in the flesh, walking the earth in order to experience the physical world and thus better understand the physical, emotional, and spiritual needs of humankind. Clearly, alas, they project onto the Blessed Messiah a quality of character that we do appreciate in the best of our human leaders, whether school principals, corporation heads, or clergy: their commitment to interacting openly with those whom they lead—teachers, employees, or members of the congregation—in order to become more knowing, able leaders. We see immediately, do we not, the flaw in their well-intended conception. They overlook the Omniness of the Tripartite Divinity. "In the beginning was the Word, and the Word was with God, and the Word was God." At that very first moment, "the beginning," which we cannot possibly imagine or comprehend, the Father, the Son, and the Holy Spirit knew and understood all that would ever be and all that would never be in the universe of universes, down to every split second in the life and bodily death of every single plant, animal, baby, girl, boy, woman, and man throughout eternity.

Perfect Rejection

So, regarding Christ's Nature and Mission on earth, we reject out of hand, do we not, the misbelief that God needed to become a literal man in order to understand humankind. Only the ignorant who misconceive the Holy Scriptures would design a Savior who, because His own strength was not sufficient, would have needed to invoke angels to assist Him. "But people who aren't spiritual can't receive these truths from God's Spirit. It all sounds foolish to them and they can't understand it, for only those who are spiritual can understand what the Spirit means" (1 Corinthians 2:14). Even though Christ said that He could call angels down or ask His

Father to send them, did He literally mean that, or was He teaching His listeners what to do if they were besieged by an overwhelming enemy? Christ needed no angels to help Him. For He Was, Is, and Always will be God the Almighty!

He that Spoke creation into existence Holds the waters of the oceans in the Palm of His Hand. The Omnipotent God, He that Parted the Red Sea and Raised the dead, is Totally Self-Sufficient. His Omnipotence empowers all lesser beings: angels, saints, pastors, and laity. Many Christians worship angels because, misguided, they have exalted them to a status perhaps even higher than that of Adonai. How shameful!

Is Not Yahweh Adonai Inscrutable and Ineffable?

In exploring the Nature of God, we have acknowledged and celebrated, have we not, the Unknowable Vast Omniness of our Actual Adonai and, as well, rejected the idea of the Buddy God, or buddy god, resulting from the secular-humanist tendency to make God manlike by projecting onto God human qualities, including fallibilities. This misguided, if well-meaning, tendency stems from people's desire to know and understand God. Some well-meaning people have said that the whole purpose of Christian theology is to search Adonai out, to know Him intimately in order to understand Him, believe in and trust Him, and follow Him. Others believe that "God in His essential nature is both inscrutable and ineffable; meaning that He is incapable of being searched into and understood;

and that He cannot tell forth or utter what He is" (Tozer,). But we know, do we not, that the Actual Adonai Is Even Greater and More Gracious than these two extreme views allow. Indeed He Is Inscrutable and Ineffable, as He must Be in order to Be God the Divine. Indeed He is not a mere Buddy God, or buddy god, created in man's image. Yet, indeed He Absolutely Makes Himself Openly Accessible to us Always. Although we cannot really know or understand Him with our rational minds, when we call for Him with all our heart, when we lean, not on our wisdom and understanding, but on our Pure Faith in Him, when we acknowledge Him each moment as our Lord and Savior, He Fills us with His Loving, Guiding Spirit. Then we *know* He is here within us, and we experience Comfort Beyond Knowing.

No doubt it is the Awesomeness of Adonai and our reverence for Him, even fear or dread of His Immeasurable Power, that have caused us to believe that such a Being is inaccessible. This human limitation is not an act of God but our susceptibility to the machinations of Satan. Such vulnerability can render us deaf to the voice of the Creator. We fail to hear God, especially when He speaks through the work of His hand, nature. We have allowed ourselves to become estranged from the knowledge that God has granted us so that we can experience, know, love, and serve God and thus live with Him in Eternity. This paucity of our own making has pulled us toward secular humanist spirituality or secular-humanist Christianity. What is that? Glorified paganism?

Adonai—may His Holy Name be praised forever!—has seemed inaccessible because, in our well-meaning efforts to glorify God as He deserves, some of us have placed Him on a celestial pedestal, distant and disconnected from our reality. We may have forgotten that God consciously "got off His Throne" and came down to affiliate with us and free us from the transience of earthly life. In doing so, God made us His spiritual children who inhabit the earth but, more importantly, will live with Him *Ad Infinitum* if we live our Faith, embrace Jesus as our Savior, and confess our sins to Him. We also may have neglected to remember that Adonai is Omnipresent and thus permeated every molecule on earth even before Christ walked it in the flesh. The Lord is Always our Lord, Always Available to Abide within us. Brethren, let us welcome Him to infuse our hearts and minds with His Divine Spirit!

Checking Our Course

As a reader of this book, you might wish, at this time, to review what you have read so far and determine how you think and feel about our journey together. The course of the book was set long before we embarked. When the course was set, all that existed "was the Word, and the Word was with God, and the Word was God" (John 1:1). If you embrace with all your heart, mind, and spirit the Truth and Worthiness of Adonai that we have been considering and proclaiming as we prepare our case for the defense, then we hope you feel motivated to continue traveling with us. Likewise, if you desire Faith and are struggling to Believe, we hope our travels aid you in fulfilling your intention. All are welcome who have an open mind and who are willing to Believe, by Faith and Truth, sustained by the Holy Spirit, that Yeshua is Lord.

We have rejected the Buddy god, misguidedly made in our human image, and we have confirmed the Infinite, Eternal Godness of Adonai. We have confirmed the Eternal Godness of Jesus the Messiah, who designed and willingly embraced His Mission on earth, including His Crucifixion. All that we have said about the Father applies as well to the Son and to the Holy Spirit. We have confirmed that, although Jesus assumed the role of a man, including body and blood, He never for a moment ceased being Divine. When we say "God," we mean "God, Jesus, and the Holy Spirit," for They are One. They are "the Word," and "the Word" is "the Holy Trinity." Steadfastly. Always.

When the Lord spoke through the psalmist King David, by design, David expressed his deepest thoughts and feelings about his experiences and his relationship with God. At times, as we have seen, he felt disconnected from God, so much so that he even felt as though God had forsaken Him. He would cry out to Adonai in prayer, begging God to forgive him for his missteps and take the sinner back into His Healing Arms. Also as we have seen, David always declared God's Constancy, Love, and Mercy. The main purpose of the Holy Scriptures is to teach us how to live godly lives. God, speaking through David, sets a fine example for us. The Psalms of David teach us honesty with ourselves and with God, the complexities of human experience, including inconstancy, loss, fear, emptiness, loneliness, and at the same time Faith in Him who is Always Here for us if we believe in Him, confess our sins, and ask Him for Forgiveness.

The Word of the Messiah

Likewise, the Words of Jesus are designed to Teach us. Everything He said, as He worked and walked among humanity, He said to Teach, Mentor, Excite, Encourage, and Inspire His followers back then and those who would follow Him thereafter. He was Teaching them and us how to live godly, connected lives, how to nurture and sustain our relationship with the Holy Trinity, how to die bravely and victoriously, and how to achieve Everlasting Life. Every single Utterance of our Lord Jesus was crafted to Teach us a Lesson, even "Father, why hast Thou forsaken me?" This seeming question may well imply as profound an answer as we might ever imagine to a question: "My Son, You know, as We wish all to know, that We never, ever break Our Word. We are Forever Constant. I am Always with You as You are Always with Me." This is the intended lesson. Jesus knew that, like King David, His disciples, when they felt themselves to be in dire straits, would ask their Father the same question. Would not the believer-followers of Christ see the death and Victorious Resurrection of our Savior as a positive message from God, assuring us that He did not forsake His son? If Christ's claims to equality or sameness with His Father should be believed, it would then be quite pertinent to ask, would God separate

Himself from Himself? That would be tantamount to One forsaking the Other!

Parsing Christ's Words?

Christ on the Cross spoke His Words aloud in His native language, Aramaic, and His Words were reported in the Holy Scriptures, most notably in Hebrew, Greek, and Latin. How did those who reported His Words know how to punctuate and indicate exactly the right emphasis, in those other languages, what Christ had said aloud in Aramaic? As well, how did those in the 16th and 17th centuries who translated the Holy Bible from those other languages into English know how to punctuate and indicate exactly the right emphasis for Christ's Words in English?

It is an essential practice in language study to "parse" sentences, which means to identify and analyze their linguistic elements. Even adding or taking away one comma can dramatically alter meaning, as in the title of a clever best-selling book by Lynn Truss on punctuation: *Eats, Shoots and Leaves* (or is it *Eats Shoots and Leaves?*). <u>Without</u> a comma after "Eats," the phrase reveals the standard diet of a panda bear. <u>With</u> a comma after "Eats," the phrase explains why, in a silly joke about faulty punctuation, a panda bear walks into a café, eats a sandwich, fires its pistol at other patrons, and walks out. Why? Because the panda had read, in the panda section of a book on wildlife, that a panda bear customarily "eats, shoots and leaves."

Parsing Christ's Words from the Cross with close attention to punctuation and emphasis reveals at least nine possibilities: (1) "<u>My</u> God, <u>My</u> God, why hast thou forsaken me?" (2) "My <u>God</u>, My <u>God</u>, why hast thou forsaken me?" (3) "My God, My God, <u>why</u> hast thou forsaken me?" (4) "My God, My God, why <u>hast</u> thou forsaken me?" (5) "My God, My God, why hast <u>thou</u> forsaken me?" (6) "My God, My God, why hast thou <u>forsaken</u> me?" (7) "My God, My God, why hast thou forsaken <u>me</u>?" (8) "My <u>God</u>? My <u>God</u>? why hast thou forsaken me?" (9) "My God, My God, <u>why</u>? Hast thou <u>forsaken</u> me?" (A number of other combinations are also possible.)

Arguably most readers of the Bible read Christ's Words as in (6) above ("My God, My God, why hast thou <u>forsaken</u> me?") with a despairing emphasis on <u>forsaken</u>. What are our two guiding principles in deciding how to punctuate, indicate exactly the right emphasis in, and interpret Christ's Words? That Jesus the Messiah Was, Is, and Always will be God with all His Omniness and that each and every Word Christ ever spoke on earth was deliberately designed to Teach us Truth. Regardless how we punctuate, indicate emphasis, and subsequently interpret Christ's utterance, we know that Christ is modeling, for His apostles and for all of us, His followers, (a) the anguish and despair and disconnection from God that, like King David, any person may experience in life and, also like King David, (b) the Steadfast Faith that God the Father, Son, and Holy Spirit are always There for us. Certainly Christ's utterance was not an indictment of Adonai.

How can people possibly believe that the Messiah—after claiming and proving every inch of the way, beyond every and all doubt, reasonable and unreasonable, that He Was and Is the Way, the Truth, the Life, and the Light of the world—how can they possibly think He would get mixed up in a reenactment of the *Tragedy of Julius Caesar* in which He plays Caesar and God the Father plays Brutus? All that is missing is not *"Et tu, Brute"* but rather *"Et tu, Abba?"* O, Lord, our God, hold not this sin against your people!

Why Did Christ Cry Out?

Surely Jesus, in all His Omniness, intentionally cried out in order to communicate a timeless message regarding the nature of human life on earth. Popular theology, alas, continues to claim, as we have seen, that our Messiah cried out because His Father, the Lord God Almighty, who had promised profusely not to forsake the righteous, had broken His promise, had forsaken Christ at the very moment of His greatest need for comfort and companionship. Why? Because Christ, in bearing all sins of the world, was no longer pure. When our Holy God, who could not look upon sin, saw His Son in such a state, He turned His back and hid His face from His Son. This big lie may sound like an excerpt from the Holy Writ, but it is not. So why have pastors, rabbis, evangelists, Bible-class teachers, and congregants been echoing this blasphemous tale for many centuries now without anyone that truly knows Adonai calling foul? In the ears of the uninitiated, it may sound like a symphony, but to those who see the Glory of Adonai, it is cacophony. Such misguided innuendo cannot stand against such scripture as "For Israel has not been widowed and forsaken, nor has Judah, by his God, the Lord of hosts, though their land is full of guilt against the Holy One of Israel" (Jeremiah 51:3)?

Pursuing the accusation that God abandoned His Christ is tantamount to painting a portrait of a God that is partial and wavering, a specter of a mere person, not the Almighty. The unscriptural presumption that God forsook Jesus has been chorused and echoed for generations, and has now become the one and only interpretation of our Lord and Master Jesus Christ's words from the Cross. There should be no doubt in our minds, as believers, as to who is sustaining this travesty, which challenges Everything that the Almighty and Eternal Sovereign Creator of the universe Was, Is, and Always Will Be. Even some believers have, perhaps inadvertently, joined the author of this lie, Satan himself, in accusing God of several perjuries and questioning His Character, His Divinity, His Essence, His Omniness.

The Nature of Sin: Rebellion against God's Instruction

We commonly use the phrase "all the sins of the world." In actuality, Christ died to free us from *the sin* of the world—*the original sin* of *disobedience* committed by Adam and Eve, from whom humanity inherited *the original sin*, including the capacity and inclination to commit further sins. This fundamental misconception regarding *the original sin* and "the sins of the world" is not insignificant and harmless. Rather, it is a noteworthy contributor to the greater misconception of what transpired at Calvary between God the Father and God the Son.

Sin, whether *the original sin* or its many derivatives, is like a poison. It affects every organ in the body before enveloping the individual in that dreaded blanket of darkness and death. When we, the general public, discuss victims of poisoning, we do not include the progression of the toxic agent through the body before it terminated the individual's earthly existence. Rather, we simply declare that they ingested or injected a poisonous substance that killed them. Only professional analysis of the cause of death produces the details of how the poison acted on the organs, tissues, and other body components to cause death.

In the same manner, theologians, both amateur and professional, often discuss sin—disobedience to God's Commandments, with its many repercussions—in a superficial way, rather than digging for the deep, "professional" truth, the root cause. We must be careful! For God must not be overlooked or mocked! Whatever we sow, that shall we also reap, and "The soul that sinned shall die," says the Lord. Those who disobey God's instructions will have to pay with their life! For example, the promiscuous, especially those who are careless, are likely to become infected by a sexually transmitted disease, which may or may not be fatal. If death should result, the medical examiners might report, as the cause, an STD. In a literal sense, they would be right. But, when promiscuity and STD's are projected against the backdrop of God's Word and viewed with God's Perspective in mind, the real cause of death should be stated as adultery or fornication. They died because they broke one of God's Commandments. The root cause was not syphilis or AIDS, but negation of and rebellion against the Laws of God. In the same way, if someone gets drunk and is involved in a fatal one-car accident, yes, being drunk cost her her life. But the fact is that she died because of her noncompliance with God's Laws. God said, "Thou shalt have no other gods before me." Those who inebriate themselves do so by praying to a buddy god: alcohol. The Lord said, "Thou shalt not kill." Those who inebriate themselves and drive make themselves potential killers. While not one of the Lord's Ten Commandments, "Don't drink and drive" is sound, godly advice for any of us who wish to follow God's Laws and live godly lives. One essential way of "knowing" the Lord is honoring His Divine Spirit within us, as people of Faith, by making godly decisions each and every moment of our lives on earth.

Popular but Depraved Interpretations

The popular but depraved interpretations of "Why hast Thou forsaken Me?" provide solid evidence that we earthlings, who are essentially spirit housed in a physical body, now walk more by sight (in the flesh) than by Faith (by the spirit). We have lent our heart to science, rationality, and empiricism. Under this very powerful influence, we have been on a wild-goose chase, attempting to capture and know merely the shadow of the Substance. We are like dogs chasing our tails. How foolish to allow ourselves to become worn down and to perish like the ant on the train track. Spiritual things are discerned spiritually! Period! And when we allow ourselves to be filled with the Divine Spirit, all manner of Wondrous Experiences await us!

Sins Were Hanging from the Body of Christ?

Brethren, let us erase that adolescent weeping-willow image from our minds. Nothing was actually hanging from the body or the Spirit of our Messiah. He was a Symbol, a Fulfillment of God's covenant with mankind. Let us think like mature, adult believers and stop sucking at beginner's milk. It must have been similar naiveté in humankind that prompted the author of the Book of Hebrews to exhort thus: "We have much to say about this, but it is hard to explain because you are slow to learn. In fact though by this time you ought to be teachers, you need someone to teach you the elementary truth of God's Word all over again" (Hebrews 5:11–12). The writer continues to encourage us: "Let us leave the elementary teachings about Christ and go on to maturity not laying again the foundations of repentance from acts that lead to death" (Hebrews 6: 1–3).

Several times through this journey so far, we have stopped to ask how this laughable concept was initiated and why it has evaded the "eyes" of spirit-filled Christians for centuries, thrived, and come to fruition. Why has it not been challenged? Why has it been "authoritatively" and "persuasively" disseminated, even by "believing" followers of Yeshua?

Honestly, Brethren, think with us. What these interpretations seem to have concluded is that, even though God is Omniscient and thus Knows Everything, He suffers lapses or amnesia. Has the *Ancient of Days* become too ancient and, therefore, out of step with the contemporary world? He Knows All Things yet, it seems, in our clouded eyes, not everything, and we, "the all knowing" humans are going to "fill Him in"? By holding on to this flawed interpretation, are we not saying that, even though God, being Omniscient, Knew that the world would reject His Commandments and consequently spill the milk, He somehow forgot to provide rags large and absorbent enough for mopping up the mess?

Each time we promote this foul teaching, which by extension questions God's Omniness, are we not saying that, when He "sent" Christ to wash away the sin of the world, unfortunately He forgot the magnitude and filthiness of the laundry that needed to be done, and because of the lapse, He was caught unawares? Indeed are we not saying that Elohim, the Almighty, is not Omniscient? Brethren, though we are still in kindergarten, we can do better than mere breast-milk-sucking babes!

Emeka Anonyuo, Ph.D.

Even My Granddaughter Amaris Knows How Much Detergent To Use

At eight years old, my granddaughter Amaris was able to estimate how much bleach or detergent was needed to do her laundry of varying colors, quantities, and qualities. Mindful of her desired end result, she successfully managed the cleaning agents, water, and settings on both the washer and dryer. If Amaris knew that much, how much more does her Heavenly Father know?

It is frightening to let one's mind glide toward the thought that God was taken unawares by the rebelliousness of His creation. Do we call this merely a simplification of God's Omniness or a devil-inspired spiting of God? What can be more criminal than casting God in the image of man or even less?

A debilitating testimony to the extreme ignorance of some Christians as to who God really is, was revealed when a preacher challenged the idea that God came down to earth to help mankind escape from the snares of the evil one. "If God came down to earth," he queried, "who was in charge of heaven in His absence?" Was he kidding? No! And he a so-called "leader" of the "faithful." Of course, as humans, we may, in our curiosity, ask such a question—so long as we answer it in the same breath: The Father, Son, and Holy Spirit have Always Been and Always Will Be In Charge of Everything Everywhere. They Always Know exactly how much detergent, bleach, and water to use, so the sun comes up each morning and sets each evening. Adonai be praised!

Adonai Does Not Forsake

Why on earth would God the Father forsake Jesus the Son when the Father had spared and not forsaken Adam and Eve, the first to rebel against His authority? He would not. Rather, He fashioned the first clothing for them after they were expelled from the Garden. This gesture establishes the absolute fact that Adonai does not forsake His children! Adam and Eve, like King David, may have felt abandoned, but the Lord never left them alone. Neither did He turn His back on Israel, who kept at her rebelliousness. Why then would God, or could God, abandon or forsake His only begotten Son, the Righteous One? God is faithful and does not renege on His promises to protect us and provide for us and not forsake us.

It is this Abiding, Enduring, Unwavering Faithfulness of God that King David sang about: "[I have] never seen the righteous forsaken." Adam and Eve were far from righteous. They had just sinned. They had just fallen short of God's Glory. Yet the Glorious One did not turn His back on them. It is the same Unparalleled, Long-Suffering Love and Faithfulness that Jeremiah 51:3 declares: "Though their land is full of guilt against the Holy One of Israel, Israel has not been widowed and forsaken, nor has Judah, by his God." If such exhibition of Divine Love is not evidence of God's Singular

Faithfulness to His Word, His Immutable Promise not to forsake His children, what is?

There must be reasons why, for millennia, the statement "Eloi, Eloi, lama sabachthani" and the multiplicity of its erroneous interpretations and explanations have romanticized, but not answered, the vital question: Did Adonai, the Blessed One, really forsake His Son, Yeshua, the Messiah?

The root causes have been explored without the inspiration and illumination of the Holy Spirit. Still—surprisingly, sadly—persistent slippery conventional explanations have satisfied spiritually unsophisticated contemporary Christians. The unsophisticated "whole truth," "the whole revelation," is yet to be granted them, which, in a nutshell, is exactly what this book is attempting to accomplish.

Believing that we need some type of conventional academic training in theology to comprehend, fully and truly, the Word of God has led to a flamboyant Christian vogue: seminary education. But does one need to be intellectually sophisticated in the ways of sanctioned conventional thinkers to understand creation and its Creator? The Book of Romans 1:13 clearly states, "No, for what the Creator intended for the creature to understand are all within creation—all around the created human being." When we slow down, become present, and actually look at our surroundings and at our fellow humans, we see—and feel—the Beauty, Power, and Glory of the Creator, in His creation.

(In "Appendices," please see "Seminary Education and Intellectual Sophistication, the Making of the 'Unholy' Bible.")

Does God Suffer Amnesia?

Yes, I have asked this question several times before and will ask it again and again: Does Adonai suffer amnesia? That is absolutely what is opined when church-goers believe the rationalists' interpretations and explanations that God suffers lapses, stutters, and prevaricates. Should church people, especially those who are sincerely seeking God, listen to the misguided postmodernist preachers who very subtly filter antichrist sentiments into the rank and file of the Church? Do believers need to do any more than believe and follow Christ, trusting in Adonai who gave His Word that He will never forsake the righteous?

Further simplified, the question reads, "Is God really God?" To answer the question correctly, we must learn what makes God God. That entails gaining clear comprehension of the Uniqueness of His Character, Divinity, and Omniness— All of Which are Manifest and Loudly Amplified in His Word and in the Works of His Hand—in creation.

God is really God, and no other gods exist with Him or beside Him. He commanded, "I am the Lord thy God . . .

Thou shall make no other god before Me nor play harlotry with alien gods made by the hands of men." Adonai is Omniscient, Omnipotent, and Omnipresent, and, very literally, the Way, Jesus Messiah. Alleluia!

That God Forsook Christ: Preachers Preach It, but Is "It" the Truth?

Again, are any of the existing proposals and allegations that Adonai forsook His Son Jesus Messiah correct? Has mankind not, in our zeal to exalt our intellectual advancement and complexity, reduced the life of Christ, His Ministry, Death, and Resurrection to mere human drama that looks more like an exaggerated fiction? Seminarians, other scholars of the Holy Bible, and, indeed, we common people, all searching and yearning for salvation and spiritual illumination—we, alas, have found this topic of Christ's crucifixion and the Passion leading to it, a fitting message for "Easter" Resurrection Sunday or Passover (*Pesach*). It is also the most favored message for publication in journals, magazines, and books for special reading during the Easter and Passover seasons.

The following excerpt from "Our Suffering Savior" (*Our Daily Bread,* July 2006) provides apt evidence of the above claim: "Father, if it be thy will, let this cup pass me by, nevertheless, not my will, but your will be done." Christ's will, as He had made it very clear, is to do the will of His Father, the One who sent Him. The article continues, "The 'cup' from which Jesus asked to be delivered from was not death. He came to die for us. I think the cup represents the frightful alienation from His Father that would lead to His cry on the cross: My God, My God, why have you forsaken me?" (Matthew 27:46, also Psalm 22:1).

The article also claims, "In the Garden, He must have anticipated that time when His Father would turn His back on Him . . . Yet, the reality of His Father's withdrawal from Him, was foremost in His thought He would be taking our sins on Himself and enduring the awesome aloneness of the cross. This realization drove Jesus to pray with so much intensity that His sweat 'became like great drops of blood'" (Luke 22:24).

Connie and I have great respect for the RBC Ministries, the publishers of the very valuable booklet, especially because their ministry significantly sustained us at the beginning stages of our walk with Adonai. We still support and receive helpful literature and electronic materials from that ministry. Unfortunately, though, because of the bogusness and immense danger that such a teaching, if uncorrected, exposes believers to, the article demands close analysis.

A Wretched Portrait of an Equivocating, Errant Divinity

The above article, a culmination of contemporary secular humanist perspective on the study of God and

His Book, presents a wretched portrait of an equivocating, waffling, flip-flopping, oscillating god. From the picture that the humanist Christians have painted of God, we see Divinity humanized and granted the frailty, the fallibility, of mankind. Jehovah Elohim has become like Peter or any of us human beings who boast about their devout, unshakable followership of the Venerable Christ but deny Him "before the cock crows."

Is God like Peter and you or me? We do not have to say directly or categorically that He waffles. All we need do, to tacitly acquiesce, is believe any part of that insipid representation of Adonai as a being susceptible to human imperfections. If we believe that Yahweh Elohim forsook His Son, we have categorically stated that He sometimes falls short of Omniscience, short of Perfection, short of Being God. Half belief is unbelief. Hot or cold, which are we? Lukewarm is not an option.

A Critical Analysis of the Article "Our Suffering Savior"

The first flaw in the article is the stereotypical status-quo perception manifest in the conventional way of looking at the Passion of the Christ, His Death, and His Resurrection. The second thing that strikes fear in a discerning Christian reader is a host of dangerous contradictions and innuendos that populate the article, the publisher's good intentions notwithstanding.

First, the article presents a Savior Who had the Ability to Foretell the future (how painful it would be "when His Father would forsake Him on the cross") and yet who later feels startled and upset by the agony of His experience. The writer fails to see the implied contradiction. Christ Was, Is, and Always Will Be the Alpha and the Omega. It is a grave mischief and insult to suggest that the Creator of the world did not know and, therefore, was not ready when the time came to be *the* Propitiation for the sin of mankind. To say that Messiah was frightened out of His wits and sweated blood and bullets at the thought of anything is to suggest that He underestimated or was completely ignorant of what lay ahead of Him. To suggest or even think such thoughts is, to put it mildly, pagan. Where is our catechism? Was not Christ born to die, not in vain, but as *the* Propitiation for the sin of the world?

The publishers exhibit genuine excitement in trying to help believing Christians understand God's Profound Love. He gave His only Son to "die" a shameful death in order to ransom captive humanity. Still, the article depicts a god who waffles, not the God we know to be Always Steadfast.

"Take This Cup Away from Me"—What Messiah Really Meant

Contrary to popular interpretations, the greater truth is that when the Venerable Christ requested that the cup be taken away, He was not really asking His Father to literally remove "the cup," which would have meant stopping the process of Salvation through His Sacrifice. What an impish, short-sighted flip-flopper mankind has made of the Messiah! Did Jesus Christ not say that He consciously and voluntarily took up the cross and could lay it down if He so desired? If the Messiah designed the whole event, choosing to offer up Himself as *the* Sacrificial Lamb for the Redemption of sinful mankind, why on earth would He plead for the abandonment of His own original plan? Indeed!

Since it is evident, from widespread misinterpretations, that mankind has all along misconstrued Who the Messiah Is and why He was "born," it is important to ask what He meant when He "requested" that "the cup" be taken away. His context cannot be understood without completing the words of His supplication: "Nevertheless, not my will, but yours be done."

So what was our Lord and Savior demonstrating? Jesus was actually teaching His apostles how to pray when strength and endurance wane. Is it not true that, after a prolonged struggle with a physical, emotional/psychological, or spiritual affliction, human strength dissipates? Such a state—wits' end—sorely tests the believer's mettle. Ask the biblical Job. Was Messiah, the Summation of the Godhead, actually being tested or tempted as some literature and movies have suggested? To insist that Christ broke down and wept blood and bullets at the thought of the conventional man-made, but Satan inspired, "separation from His Father" is to strip Him of His Divinity, His place within the Godhead, and to miss one of the most important Lessons of the Holy Scriptures.

Remember that the cross of Christ was not forced upon Him. All the mighty armies of ancient Rome, combined with the influence of the quibbling Sanhedrin, would have paled at the Power of the Lord, if He had so willed. But the Sacrificial Lamb willingly placed Himself upon the altar. He took the Cross by choice and openly declared that, if He pleased, He could lay it down—His point being that, Willingly, He *Chose* not to lay it down.

Our Master Yeshua Messiah willingly and knowingly did what He did. Nothing took Him by surprise—not the Cross, not the roles played by Pilate, Herod, the Chief priest and Sanhedrin, Simon of Cyrene, or Joseph of Arimathea, and not the words that were spoken or actions that were initiated by the designated actors. Remember, also, that our Lord forewarned Peter about his denial and Judas about his betrayal. None of those took Him unawares. Why? Because He Wrote the script, Made the actors, Designed the props and set, courtrooms, Golgotha, and all. Remember that "all that were made, were made by Him, and that without Him, nothing that was made would have been made" . Brethren, He is Adonai Yeshua, and Nothing Is Impossible with Him. Let us always praise Him!

We Invite You, Brethren, to Step Away from the Convention, Bury the Clichés, and Join in Our Journey to Truth, the Whole Godly Truth

Omniscient: Adonai Is or He Is Not

Certain vital questions must be asked and re-asked. Is God Omniscient, or is He not? Did He make provision for the cleansing of mankind's sinful nature before the fall of Adam and Eve, or did He not? Does the Creator of the universe simply ad lib His way through unexpected occurrences, some of which startle Him because of their magnitude and suddenness? Is anything impossible for God? Anything? My friends, we children of the Most High, we must not waffle in this crucial examination. We must not compromise our beliefs. There is no middle ground. Either Adonai is Immutable, or He is a mere demigod. Between the two extremes is a yawning, all-consuming chasm. Let us not be misled by the false concept of purgatory. Such makes nonsense of "I have placed before you life and death, good and evil, heaven and hell, God and the Devil, choose you one" (Deuteronomy 30:15). The idea of purgatory also defies Revelations 3:13: "I wish that you were hot or cold, and because you are neither, I will spit you out of my mouth." We must be one or the other, not one and the other. We must stand in one or the other camp, heaven or hell, not in between, for there is no place like that. It is an imaginary place created by those who bury Original Truth with quasi truths.

As we have seen, a principal reason for our pilgrimage is to analyze honestly and truthfully the crucial utterance "*Eloi Eloi, lama sabbactani*" with a mind to unveiling what has been shrouded for centuries. In His Sermon on the Mount, Jesus said to His disciples and followers,

You are the salt of the earth; but if salt has lost its taste, how can its saltiness be restored? It is no longer good for anything, but is thrown out and trampled under foot. You are the light of the world. A city built on a hill cannot be hidden. No one after lighting a lamp puts it under the bushel basket, but on the lampstand, and it gives light to all in the house. In the same way, let your light shine before others, so that they may see your good works and give glory to your Father in heaven. (Matthew 5:13-16)

Brethren let us be both salt and light. Let us join many other positive builders in reconstructing the Body of Christ. Let us help correct the gross misunderstanding that has for too long misrepresented the Almighty God as a mere demigod. We know the truth, do we not: He Is Omnipotent, Omniscient, Omnipresent, Immutable, Good, Just, and Worthy. Glory and Honor and Power Belong to Him Forever and Ever! Amen.

Detractors Mask as Agents of the Kingdom

It has become increasingly difficult for mankind to believe in and follow after Jesus Messiah. Detractors, masking as agents of the Kingdom, place obstacles in our paths. Attempting to escape from materialism, we seek the transcendent life of the spirit. Our adversaries strive to keep us apart from Christ by spreading lies about the Holy One, by questioning the very Omniness of *HaShem*, our Blessed

Master. Somehow, secular humanism, like the crafty serpent in Eden, has slithered even into the churches and devoured the unsuspecting chicks huddled in the pews. Humanism's fashionable postmodernism descries our very Godhead. These secular humanists and, as well, many professed Christians actually believe and teach that our Creator did not create all things and does not know all things. In fact, they claim that God is really man, who can outdo God. In their warped minds, they trim God down to man size and strip Him of His Divinity. They are midgets attempting to bring down a Towering Giant.

A good boxer knows how to make up for a differential in height or brawn. He throws powerful, punishing punches to the midsection of the taller opponent, causing him to bend forward into reach. How has mankind adopted this strategy? By reducing the Word of God to mere suggestions or proposals. Take for example these words by our Venerable Messiah: "No man knows when the Lord has chosen to come again, not even the Angels" (Matthew 24:36). Theologians insist upon disagreeing with these words of Jesus, claiming to know otherwise. They have written thousands of books and articles that assign clear, inflexible dates and times for the *Second Coming* of the Lord. Do you wish to write a best-seller? Simply muster the courage to fault Adonai. Simply think up new ways to challenge His Omniness and to lead your readers down yet another path to self-destruction.

Generally speaking, mankind has grown weary of hearkening to the counsel, the wisdom of the Holy Bible.

These miserable beings, though saddled with sins of many colors, have taken up with leaders who have, for fleeting political fame, excised life-saving, life-sustaining Truths from the Word of God. Political contestants draw tumultuous applause from their doting, sometimes bemused or hypnotized, admirers by amending the Commandments given to us by our Creator.

Let these words ring in the ears of those who challenge the Might of El Shaddai, the One True God: "How can you call me Master when you do not obey my Commandments?" (Luke 6:46). "With your lips you praise me, but your heart is far away from me" (Isaiah 29:13). How can the sheep shepherd the shepherd? See, in our stubbornness and foolhardiness, we have put the cart before the horse—our own will and presumptuous intelligence before God's Will. Now, see how well we are doing. After amending our nation's constitution, tailoring it to the hearts of secular humanists, we become so emboldened as to take aim at the very Commandments of God, with a mind to excise those that make us uncomfortable.

A Prayer

O proud man and woman, should you now put the Lord, your God, to the test? Should you now tempt Him? Give us godly wisdom, O Lord, our God, for our jaundiced mind is leading us astray. Light our paths that we may see. For our eyes have been dimmed by clouds rising from the strange sacrifices that we have offered up to strange, false deities. Revive us again, O Glorious One, that we may be remade and found worthy by the Savior of our souls if He should return tonight. Amen.

Chapter 3

THE TRIAL

Does God Forsake the Righteous? Did He Forsake Christ at Calvary, Resulting in the Cry, "My Lord, My Lord, Why Have You Forsaken Me?"

Presenting the Actors and Their Actions

The main charges are that God equivocates and forsakes us, even after He promised not to, and that He forsook Yeshua Messiah as He hung on the cross. The counter-charge we proclaim is unflinching: **God does not forsake, never has forsaken, and never will forsake the righteous. Period! More importantly, He did not forsake His Son, our Messiah.** We unequivocally reject the conventional interpretations given to "My God, why have you forsaken Me?" We summarily dismiss the generally held interpretations, which were designed in hell to deceive and distract those of us who have pure Faith in God's Will and who try to walk the path of righteousness.

Brethren, let us guard our hearts and minds. If we provide Satan with the slightest opening, even a pinhole, the snake will slither through like a chilly winter's gust. Being aware of his craftiness and determination, we are making sure, in presenting this book, that we do not allow zeal, dogma, or orthodoxy to cloud the Truth. We much appreciate and carefully employ the shields that Adonai provides for our spiritual safety.

To help us answer the vital questions raised above concerning the Omniness and Immutability of Adonai, we will explore the cycle of life, highlighting natural laws, scientific laws, and other realities. We will explore causes and effects, how actions birth reactions. And we will explore what civilizations have called natural justice, involving karmic laws, laws of retribution, as in "what goes around, comes around." A simple "biblical" way of saying this is "The soul that sins shall die" because the Lord will ask all men and women to give account of their stewardship. We will encapsulate vast biblical events in a handful of representative occurrences, whether initiated by God or humans. Quoted verses of the Holy Bible are not arranged chronologically but are grouped to represent people's actions, namely rebellion and disobedience, that precipitated God's reaction.

The People's Rebellious Actions: Forsaking God

This section explores people's actions that triggered God's reactions—which, erroneously, have been viewed as His abandonment of His people. The segment seeks to answer the question, What did the people do and say that went contrary to the Commandments of God and that consequently necessitated God's "reaction," often seen as God's punishment or rejection of His people? It is important to understand that the alleged passivity of God does not amount to His doing anything but in certain contexts suggests an act of Humble Submission to the will of the people.

> I have been very jealous for the Lord God of hosts; for the Israelites have forsaken Your covenant, thrown down Your altars, and killed Your prophets with the sword. And I, I only, am left; and they seek my life, to take it away. (1 Kings 19:10)

> They offer to the Lord every morning and every evening burnt sacrifices and incense of sweet spices; they set in order the showbread on the table of pure gold and attend to the golden lamp stand, that its lamps may be lighted every evening. For we keep the charge of the Lord our God, but you have forsaken Him. (2 Chronicles 13:11; Jeremiah 1:16)

> For our fathers have trespassed and have done what was evil in the sight of the Lord our God and they have forsaken Him and have turned away their faces from the dwelling place of the Lord and have turned their backs. (2 Chronicles 29:6)

> Then said He to me, Son of man, have you seen what the elders of the house of Israel do in the dark, every man in his [secret] chambers of [idol] pictures? For they say, The Lord does not see us; the Lord has forsaken the land. (Ezekiel 8:12)

Emeka Anonyuo, Ph.D.

If God had forsaken the land as the people alleged, why should He care about what was going on in the house of Israel? It is true that, before God punished a people in the past, and He does the same in our time, He would let one of His servants, a prophet, know ahead of time so that the erring people would be warned. This way, God intends to offer the people an opportunity to repent and be forgiven. Remember God's dialogue with Abraham before Sodom and Gomorrah were consumed. Recall also the conversation between Samuel and King Saul concerning the Amalekites, the argument of Elijah and Ahab/Jezebel, and more. Those who still hear His voice insist that God still speaks today as clearly as He spoke in the days of the Torah.

Forsaken versus the Fear of Being Forsaken

In the Book of Ruth, it is recorded that Naomi, fearing the Lord had abandoned her (the reason for the many calamities that had befallen her), asked that her name be changed to Mara, meaning "bitter." The question is, did God abandon Naomi? The answer is no. Why then did she feel forsaken? Because of the many calamities that had befallen her, the very reason why contemporary Christians feel abandoned or betrayed by God. The state of uncertainty that eventually produces lingering doubts about God's willingness to invest His time in mankind's affairs can be witnessed in the life of John the Baptist. Yes, John, having been granted divine revelation of who the Messiah was, had said that John was not qualified to untie the lace of His sandals. Does one need a terminal degree in theology/Christology and need to become adept in cryptology to be able to understand the speakers' conviction? After all, he was Prophet extraordinaire.

But someone would ask, in fact many have asked, why, later on, the Baptizer sent his disciple to Jesus Christ to ask specifically whether Christ was the one whom John had been preaching about. What happened? The same John who identified Christ as the Messiah—why was he suddenly uncertain? Many answers can be postulated. But what stands out most prominently is that, because John had suffered many negative occurrences in his life, and his cousin, the Messiah, had not come to his assistance, his faith eroded, causing him to seek signs. As his faith ebbed, he sought practical, literal proof. To the inquirers sent by John, the Messiah said, "Go tell him what your eyes have seen." The truth is that no empirical proof is needed. We walk by faith, not by sight!

Have you ever been tempted to believe, as Naomi did and John may have suspected, that Adonai has forgotten you simply because your supplications or expectations were not met on time, according to your schedule?

It is important to differentiate between being forsaken and the fear or feeling of having been forsaken. When we suspect that God has forsaken us, it is almost always the paralyzing, even morbid, fear of impending punishment or doom that generates our organ-churning emotional response. In the case of the Israelites, for example, when the rebels became fully aware, not only of their vulnerability, but also of their guilt, they did what comes naturally to most human beings: pass the buck by blaming a subordinate or high-handed boss. The Israelites blamed Adonai. King Saul did not feel the full impact of the spirit of melancholy until his disobedience was published. Usually, we do not feel truly abandoned until we are confronted by negative events or else reprimanded, chastised, or rebuked directly by God, or through His Prophet, or by the Holy Spirit, the Spirit of Conviction, concerning our misdeeds.

When this happens, we naturally feel anxiety, a nervous state that finally births the psychological experience of forsakenness. The truth is that this feeling is not of God. For He offers only the Power of Love and Sound Mind, never fear or debilitating imaginings. Adonai is never further from us than we think He is. God is our Ever-Present Friend who sticks closer than a brother or sister. "For they say, The Lord does not see us; the Lord has forsaken the land" (Ezekiel 8:12). Where was God at the time of that statement? In Heaven, conducting a conference? Or cut off by a dark cloud of disobedience, perhaps idolatry? Did He momentarily lose His Omnipresence? Is *Jehovah Shammah*, the Lord Who Is Always Here, not here all the time?

Failing to find a satisfactory way to describe Adonai's attitude towards sin, considering especially His Indescribable Immaculate Purity, we, in our zeal, project onto God mortal characteristics, often withdrawing from our adversaries when provoked. Adonai is slow to anger; His long-sufferingness sustaining His desire to see that all men come to the saving knowledge of His Word, Yeshua Messiah, and be perfected.

If God withdraws His presence at the very first exhibition of mankind's disobedience, how was He able to see and describe the progression of the people's disobedience to Prophet Ezekiel? For example, in Ezekiel's vision, the Lord showed him "the detestable to the utterly detestable to even more detestable things" that the elders did in the temple: "Son of man, look toward the north, I did and saw the idol that provokes jealousy. And the Lord said to me; do you see what they are doing; the utterly detestable things that the House of Israel is doing, things that will drive me far from my sanctuary. But you will see things that are even *more detestable*" (Ezekiel 8:22); (emphasis mine). For more detestable practices, read Ezekiel 8:9–11: "Do you see what the elders of Judah are doing in the darkness, each at the temple of his own idol"? There the Lord showed him about twenty-five elders of Israel sitting with their backs toward God's temple and their faces toward the east, bowing down to the sun. "Will you fill the land with violence and continually provoke me to anger?" asked the Lord.

Adonai Sees and Knows all things. His long-suffering Patience enables Him to Watch all our deeds until He can bear no more and "turns His face away." This action does not mean that He becomes unaware or that He withdraws His Mercy and Love and Grace from us.

Emeka Anonyuo, Ph.D.

God's Reaction to Acts of Disobedience

The Lord said to Ezekiel, "Son of man, see what they are doing; the utterly detestable things that the House of Israel is doing, *things that will drive me far from my sanctuary* (Ezekial 8:6; emphasis mine). In Ezekiel 8:18, the Lord says, 'I will deal with them in anger; I will not look on them with pity . . . I will not listen to them even if they shout in my ears."

"The Lord shall send you curses, confusion, and rebuke in every enterprise to which you set your hand, until you are destroyed, perishing quickly because of the evil of your doings by which you have *forsaken me*" (Deuteronomy 28:20; emphasis mine). Who had forsaken whom?

The people's fear was anticipatory. They had already judged themselves and found themselves guilty of forsaking the Lord's instructions. God had not forsaken them, but the provocative rebellious actions of the people had warranted God's cautionary reaction. "The Lord shall" speaks about future action that may or may not be undertaken. Again, I hurriedly state that, when God casts aside someone who has acted from a reprobate mind and heart, He is done with such a subject. At the same time, if He follows up a threat with chastisement or punishment, then He is steering the erring person back to Himself.

It is not hard to figure out from the above quotation that it was the people who did the *forsaking*; God's reaction did not produce the people's action, but vice versa. As a matter of fact, God did not and does not need to forsake someone who has already forsaken Him. If one is rejected by a friend or spouse, the rejected party does not need to reject back. She or he does not have a choice—but is simply a reject. The following quotation contains a telling redundancy: "Because you have forsaken the Lord, He also has forsaken you" (2 Chronicles 24:20).

They have forsaken the Lord, and that's it. God does not have to do anything. He does not need to reject anyone. He does not need that choice. It would amount to childishness if those who have been rejected say to the offender, "I also reject you." The only choice open to them is to love those who have forsaken them, and this is what God does always, especially after we have repented of our rebelliousness against Him. His Love, Mercy, and Goodness Endure Forever, whether we love Him or hate Him. This explains why Adonai Yeshua, our Father and Perfect Example, commands and expects us to love those who hate and misuse us. Think on this for a moment: how can, and why should, God expect us to love those who hate and deride us, if He is incapable of doing the same? The problem for those who hate the Lord is that their hate or disobedience beclouds or completely blinds and desensitizes them to the Presence, the Love, and the Goodness of Adonai. Are you thinking with us?

In the above redundant statement, "Because you have forsaken the Lord, He also has forsaken you" (2 Chronicles 24:20), the prophet was only using words to explain to the people who were spiritually hard of hearing why things were falling apart for them. They knew when God took His Hand away, but it was always difficult for them to ascertain the cause of the consequence.

Remember Samuel's prophetic words to King Saul: "Why do you consult me, now that the Lord has departed from you and become your enemy? The Lord has done what he predicted through me. The Lord has torn the kingdom out of your hands and given it to one of your neighbors—to David. Because you did not obey the Lord or carry out his fierce wrath against the Amalekites, the Lord has done this to you today" (1 Samuel 16-18). The prophet was using these words to help the listener understand what was happening to him. God did not have to actually rip the crown from or reject King Saul. First, Saul was not God's choice. Second, King Saul rejected the Lord through crass disobedience to the simple instructions given to him by HaShem. Third, God did not kill King Saul. Rather Saul committed suicide. Let us not suspect that God sent an evil spirit to Saul, for such a thought would be blasphemous.

The devil, never God, sends evil spirits. Disobedience to God's Instruction is obedience to Satan's twisted orders. The human mind and heart abhor vacuum. Either God or Satan must be in residence, but never at the same time, for they do not co-exist. So, when King Saul disobeyed Adonai, he welcomed Satan into his life, by choice. God did not forsake King Saul. Rather, God sustained him even though Saul was not His choice from the onset. Saul abandoned Almighty God by disobeying Him. King Saul compounded a very volatile situation, failure to carry out instructions against King Agag and the Amalekites, by choosing to sacrifice to God, thus usurping the office of the chief priest, rather than obeying God. Hence the rebuke by Samuel: "Obedience is better than sacrifice" (1 Samuel 15:22).

Offender (Israel) Thought That the Offended (Adonai) Was Guilty

Let us see another instance where offenders (the people) mistook the offended (Adonai) as the guilty one. "Then the Spirit of God came upon Zechariah, son of Jehoiada the priest, who stood over the people, and he said to them, thus says God: Why do you transgress the commandments of the Lord so that you cannot prosper? Because you have forsaken the Lord, He also has forsaken you" (2 Chronicles 24:20). The key point is "because you have forsaken the Lord, He also has forsaken you." Did God have a choice in the matter? God did not abandon the people; the people abandoned Him.

Remember that the message was delivered by a third-person speaker, not directly by God. The prophet tried to explain to the bewildered gathering the reasons for their situation: "You people turned your back on God, and apparently He respected and accepted your decision." Does that not sound pertinent? What would you have done if you were in God's position? Would you have done what He did, still loved them but allowed them to come to their senses and make amends? "He who watches over Israel never slumbers or sleeps" (Psalm 121:4) even when Israel does. *Baruch HaShem*. Praise His Name.

Forsake? God Does Not Have a Back to Turn on People

This thought may sound comical or ridiculous, but the truth is that God never turns His back because technically He has no back, not even a metaphorical one. He is an All-Pervading Presence. Let us keep that in mind the next time we read or hear a discourse on "Eli Eli lama sabachthani." Elohim is Spirit, and those who worship and fellowship with Him accomplish those in and through the spirit of Truth.

In summary, we do not reject ourselves because others have rejected us, nor do we reject those who have rejected us. Why? Because Adonai instructs us to love such people. The truth is that, if we have been abandoned, we do not have a choice to return the favor. Our adversaries are no longer existent in our reality. If we dialed their phone numbers, they would not pick up. If people walk away from us, we do not need to walk away from them—we are already separated from them, whether we move or not. Adonai does not change address. Ask the prodigal son.

As It Was With the Prodigal Son

The parable of the prodigal son teaches that when we break God's Commandments, we separate ourselves from Him. Our separation does not cause Him to move away from where He, the Immovable Presence, has been since before the foundation of the universe. If, as erring children, we ever come back to where we separated ourselves from our Heavenly Father, we will find Him exactly where we left Him, for He is Always Everywhere. After the prodigal son had harvested the fruits of his rebellion, he knew exactly where home was. His GPS was the voice and love of his father. The address was the same, as the prodigal son found out when the spiritual GPS announced, "Now arriving at your destination." Of course, his separation from his father had been physical as well as intellectual and emotional. Since God is Always Everywhere, when we break from Him, we separate ourselves from Him spiritually, intellectually, and emotionally, but not physically.

Forsaking Adonai: How Do We Alienate Ourselves from God?

Friendship with the world, which is to say worldliness, is enmity with Adonai. One is separated from Yeshua Adonai through disobedience. Any act of rebellion against God, no matter how trivial or minimized, becomes a significant step away from God, from Home. If this rebellion continues, the heart may become calloused, causing the individual to become so steeped in and eclipsed by evil that he or she is no longer sensitive to the presence of the Holy Spirit, even when that presence is overwhelming. When we forsake the safety of our bomb shelter, our hiding place, our strong tower, we are exposed to the hazards of a bomb blast. Our foolishness and wrong choices are responsible for our demise. What kills us is our insubordination. The bomb, as a mere instrument of destruction, only puts the finishing touches on our choice to die. "Your sins will find you out" becomes a true statement because eventually, as the Lord spoke through the Prophet Jeremiah,

> your own wickedness shall chasten and correct you, and your backslidings and desertion of faith shall reprove you. Know therefore and recognize that this is an evil and bitter thing: [first,] you have forsaken the Lord your God; [second,] you are indifferent to Me and the fear of Me is not in you, says the Lord of hosts. (Jeremiah 2:19)

The Lord again makes it clear that, although people go through many negative experiences, it is not God who engineers them. Adonai, blessed be His Name, does not condemn or destroy, and neither does He author the agencies that cause them. No, the Lord says, "Your own wickedness shall chasten and correct you, and your backslidings and desertion of faith shall reprove you" (Jeremiah 2:19).

Brethren, common sense concurs with the Holy Scriptures: only those who hear the Voice of God and fear

Him seek and achieve Forgiveness and Salvation. That is the only reason why our Loving, Generous Heavenly Father allows us to experience the consequences of our rebellion against His instructions. It would be pertinent to ask, Okay, who sends people to hell? How about Sodom and Gomorrah?

Adonai Does Not Send Anyone to Hell

Jeremiah 2:19 should also help us understand that God does not send anyone to hell. *Our own choices* chart our course in life. We travel either God's avenue through the narrow gate or Satan's expressway through the wide gate. Let us choose today whom we will serve, Adonai or Satan, Yeshua or Beelzebub. There is no in-between. So we see, brothers and sisters, that the choice is ours, not God's, and our choice determines the nature of our life for now and for eternity.

Forsaking People Is Not God's Style

Prophet Shemaiah's message proves once more that to forsake is not God's way. Shemaiah came to Jeroboam and the princes of Judah, who had gathered at Jerusalem because of *Shishak*, and said to them, "Thus says the Lord: **You have forsaken Me**, so I have abandoned you into the hands of Shishak" (2 Chronicles 12: 5; emphasis mine)

God had no choice. He held up a Shield that protected anyone who listened to His instructions to take shelter behind it. People consciously exposed themselves to the enemy, not because God removed the Shield, but because they were rebellious, and like shifting sand, drifted from the shadow of the Almighty. When the mind is reprobate, the Lord gives one over, for the Lord said that His spirit will not contend with the spirit of man forever. The Lord's act of giving the persistent sinner over to a reprobate mind simply means that He lets that person's choice prevail. It is this character of God that has made it extremely difficult for many to understand His Love and Mercy. Wish to see and experience absolute freedom of choice? Try Adonai.

Abandoning the Lord's Umbrella

This matter is reminiscent of an event on one stormy day in Savannah, Georgia. As I waited for the bus to arrive at the stop, a violent wind wrestled a half-shredded umbrella from the hands of a feeble old woman cuddling her granddaughter. I did not have a moment to think, and three steps brought me to the couple with whom I intended to share my meager shelter—my umbrella. Without a word, she backed up three steps into the rain, and as she did so, slipped on wet trash and fell. Puzzled by her sudden movement away from me, I spent a few seconds wondering if I should help them up.

My love of Christ did move me to assist them. I did not feel bad, having assumed that her action was inspired by racism, or by a well-meaning attempt to protect her granddaughter from "that bearded stranger," or both.

Who knows how or why such an elderly woman had come to be the apparent caretaker of that child. I can only guess that the child's teenage mother may have fallen victim to the insatiable lechery in our promiscuous contemporary society. Perhaps the grandmother was simply insulating her granddaughter from the fallout of our world, where evil is exalted while a few good people read their Bibles and mind their own business. I just wondered and, yes, felt pity for the child. As for the grandmother, she made a choice. She was responsible for her apparent fear of me, and her jumping back brought about her fall. Our actions always generate reactions and consequences. Always.

Forsaking Adonai: Unrelenting Flirtation with Strange Gods

In reaction to the unrelenting flirtation with strange cultures, HaShem was provoked to declare, "They shall eat and not have enough; they shall play the harlot and beget no increase, because they have **forsaken the Lord** for harlotry" (Hosea 4:10).

Why do they eat and not have enough? Because they have gone beyond flirting with alien gods and are now actually frolicking with them. What husband or wife stays married to a spouse who has sexual liaisons with others? Unlike mankind, God shows His long-suffering Love and Faithfulness. He commanded Hosea to stay married to a prostitute. Adonai was prepared to keep His people from utter destruction. He did not forget or forsake them even though they thought that He did. The Israelites had a multitude of reasons to believe and expect that Adonai would justifiably rain brimstone on them.

If God's "I will deliver you no more" means exactly that, why did Yeshua come? Why did Adonai prepare a Lamb that would be slain for our redemption He declares, **"I will never leave you nor forsake you even if your parents do . . . I will be with you even to the end of time"**. Yet those whom He protects accuse Him of prevarication.

It is hard to understand the ways of Adonai simply because His ways are not mankind's ways. We experience this mysteriousness when we attempt to paint an accurate portrait of God and His dealings with us. Our confusion comes from the fact that, after Adonai expresses disgust at our wicked ways, He still protects and provides for us. For example, we might well suspect that God might abandon us when we read, "Even though you have forsaken Me and served other gods; therefore I will deliver you no more. Go and cry out to the gods you have chosen. Let them save you when you are in trouble." But listen as the benevolent Adonai continues, almost pleadingly, "But if My people that are called by name shall humble themselves, repent of their sins and turn away from their wicked ways, then shall I hear their supplication, and heal their land" (Judges 10:13–14).

Who did the forsaking? The people did, and not God. Father was simply reminding them that, since they rejected

His protective arm, He was going to allow them to move on. Honestly, God's statement that He would not deliver them anymore was not necessary, because the people had already asked Him not to deliver them. Why? Because they had found another "deliverer" in the strange deities they now served. It is difficult to understand why detractors have cried out against God, accusing Him of contradictions or of waffling and tripping over His Word.

God's intention for allowing us to partially reap the fruit of our silliness is basically to get rebellious mankind to the point of repentance and contrition so that He can restore us. When God acquiesced to the people's choice of another deliverer, something in His announcement made the listeners uncomfortable and triggered a quick confession. "Lord," they chorused, "we have sinned. Do with us whatever you think best. But please rescue us now." After this confession and resolution to serve the Lord, they abandoned their foreign gods among them and served Adonai—exactly what Adonai intended. In secular life, we would call that temporary cessation, withdrawal of affection or love, to get a child's attention, with a positive outcome in mind.

"You Shall Have No Other Gods before Me": Kindling God's Wrath

Let us review this statement and confirm that it was the people who constantly forsook God through their disobedience and spiritual prostitution. The Lord's stance was a necessary reaction to a persistent infraction. The most important Commandment and, unfortunately, the most broken is the first of the Ten: "You shall have no other gods before Me." If this one Law is broken, the rest fall apart, and so is our harmonious cooperative existence with the Sprit of God.

> Because they have forsaken Me and have burned incense to other gods [Since they chose to walk away from the shelter], provoking Me to anger with all the work of their hands, therefore [they will be drenched by acid rain and exposed to the curses which come with it]. My wrath will be kindled against this place and will not be quenched. (2 Kings 22:17)

What is God's wrath, and how is it kindled against a people or a place? What is called the wrath of God is actually His being democratic and respectful of our choices and His allowing us, by our own choice, to drift away from the Shield, from the Wall of Safety that He has built around us. He may do this to allow us to be tested or chastised. Remember Job. Why did he go through all those unnamable, dreadful times? Did God cause all that suffering? Or did he allow it to be perpetrated by Satan for some basic reason much greater than merely to see Job suffer? Could God have stopped Job's ordeal? Did He? We can say with confidence that Job himself stopped his ordeal. For the first time in his life, he actually looked at, "saw," listened to, and heard God. Voila! His tribulations ended! The "battle" for Job's soul was over. Did

Satan ever show up to capitulate to God and congratulate Him for winning Job's faithfulness? Of course not!

Contrary to Conventional Wisdom, Adonai Is Incapable of Doing Evil

The point of this argument is to show that God is not capable of anything bad, evil, destructive, or unpleasant, even if such were to happen as a result of mankind's rebellion, as in the case of the Israelites. Besides having to roam the wilderness for approximately forty years, the Israelites experienced some of the most horrifying outcomes of their rebellion and constant complaints against God and His servant Moses. Unfortunately, those outcomes have all been blamed on Adonai and counted against Him as equivocation on His promises to protect His chosen people.

Forsaking Adonai is Spiritual Suicide

This takes us back to "Because you have forsaken me, I have also forsaken you." Forsaking God, in all its definitions and ramifications, is a foolish and suicidal act; it is like walking the tightrope across the Grand Canyon without a harness or allowing a toddler to toy with a primed grenade. This suicidal act involves our slowly drifting, consciously or unconsciously, away from the Protective Wall that our Divine Father builds around us. The following passage can help us understand what transpires after mankind forsakes

God, our shelter and strong tower in times of trouble: "Your own wickedness shall chasten and correct you, and your backslidings and desertion of faith shall reprove you. Know therefore and recognize that this is an evil and bitter thing: [first,] you have forsaken the Lord your God; [second,] you are indifferent to Me and the fear of Me is not in you, says the Lord of hosts" (Jeremiah 2:19).

"They sow the wind," the Holy Scriptures caution, "and reap the whirlwind" (Hosea 8:7). It is true that such harvests come multiplied a hundredfold. One kernel of corn will produce many cobs with hundreds of kernels. Some people associate this concept of sowing and reaping with Karmic law or the law of retribution. Not even King David, Moses, Aaron, Samson, and many other chosen men and women of God escaped the tentacles of the natural law of justice.

Every action, be it good or bad, leaves a reaction in its wake. What is our reaction at harvest time?

So we see that God does not have to do anything to bring about pain because, as soon as we step out from the shadow of the Almighty, we are in the full glare of the enemy, Satan. Remember that God does not tempt but tests; the testing of our faith produces endurance, not disaster. He sends or allows testing to grant us the opportunity to show how much we have learned from Him and trusted Him and to prove to the enemy, when he tempts us, that we are God's children. That delights God and should exhilarate us as His children.

Adonai Is Doing This Terrible Thing for No Reason? Even Gideon Thought So

When we lose sight of the connection between our disobedience to the Commandments of God and the strange things happening to us as a result, we surmise—as did Gideon—that for no reason at all, God is doing these terrible things to us.

The brave Gideon exhibited mankind's frail understanding of God and upheld the unfair expectation that God is obliged unconditionally and continually to bless us, no matter what. Listen in to Gideon's dialogue with an angel of the Lord: "The Lord is with you mighty warrior," said the Angel. Gideon replied, "O sir, if the Lord is with us, why is all this befallen us? And where are all His wondrous works of which our fathers told us, saying, Did not the Lord bring us up from Egypt? But now the Lord has forsaken us and given us into the hand of Midian" (Judges: 6:13). Pastor Johnson presented Gideon's response more comically: "O yaw, tell me something else, angel. I actually doubt that you are original because you should have known the truth. How can you stand there and tell me that, that . . . [pause] He is with us, and we can hardly count our dead, nor find enough vacant plots of land to bury them?"

Is it not surprising that even Gideon, who was specifically chosen and had walked with the Lord, would be astonished at the estrangement of the people and at God's "reaction?"

Emeka Anonyuo, Ph.D.

Prophet Isaiah, seemingly advocating for God, provides the answer:

> A people loaded with iniquity, offspring of evildoers, sons who deal corruptly! They have forsaken the Lord, they have despised and shown contempt and provoked the Holy One of Israel to anger, and they have become utterly estranged from God. (Isaiah 1:4)

Prophet Isaiah has it right. "They have forsaken the Lord"; that is why "now the Lord has forsaken us and given us into the hand of the Midian" (Judges 6:13). So we see again that it was not God that did the forsaking. Please note Prophet Isaiah's way of stating what was happening to the people: "People loaded down with iniquity . . . they have become utterly estranged from God." Isaiah did not say that God had separated Himself from His people. Remember that the prophet was not making up his own words but writing with power and authority as the Spirit of God Spoke into his heart. He was not a twenty-first-century, self-proclaimed or man-made prophet, whose empty words are sanitized so as not to offend the "spoiled" congregants as they unashamedly carouse in the cursed embrace of secular humanism.

No, Prophet Isaiah advocates for the Lord: 'Surely You have rejected and forsaken your people, the house of Jacob, because they are filled [with customs] from the east and with soothsayers [who foretell] like the Philistines; also they strike hands and make pledges and agreements with the children of aliens" (Isaiah 2:6, also Deuteronomy 18:9–12).

I Will Never Forsake You: Adonai's Unfailing Promise

God promised not to forsake the righteous, and His Word being His Bond, He Watches it closely to bring it to fulfillment. With God, His Word will always be made flesh—made real—and dwell among His people. Who are these people, the people of God for whom the sovereign Lord provides? And what are His expectations of them? "If My people who are called by my Name, would humble themselves, pray, turn from their wicked ways and seek My face, then will I hear their supplication, and visit them and heal their land" (2 Chronicles 7:14).

After repeating causes and effects of our actions, we do not need a theology class to understand that it is really not God but "your own wickedness [that] shall chasten and correct you, and your backslidings and desertion of faith shall reprove you. Know therefore and recognize that this is an evil and bitter thing: [first] you have forsaken the Lord your God; [second] you are indifferent to Me and the fear of Me is not in you, says the Lord of hosts" (Jeremiah 2:19).

Such passages should help us review the common misconception of what God means by "And I will utter My judgments against them for all the wickedness of those who have forsaken Me, burned incense to other gods, and worshiped the works of their own hands" (Jeremiah 1:16). "For My people have committed two evils: they have forsaken Me, the Fountain of living waters, and they have hewn for themselves cisterns, broken cisterns which cannot hold water" (Jeremiah 1:13). "Why should I and how can I pass over this and forgive you for it? Your children have forsaken Me and sworn by those that are no gods. When I had fed them to the full and bound them to Me by oath, they committed [spiritual] adultery, assembling themselves in troops at the houses of [idol] harlots" (Jeremiah 5:7).

How many times did the people expect the Lord to explain His action and reactions? The major duty of the prophets was to tell the people what Adonai was saying to them and to warn them about their impending doom should they fail to hearken to God's instructions. Primarily, the prophets warned against forsaking the Lord and told them the dreadful things that awaited them should they turn their back on God. Because the Almighty was not going to give up on His chosen people, He continually explained things to them, as He does here through Jeremiah: "And when your people say, Why has the Lord our God done all these things to us? Then you shall answer them, as you have forsaken Me, says the Lord, and have served strange gods in your land, so shall you serve strangers [demi-gods] in a land that is not yours" (Jeremiah 5:19).

The summary remains the same: "Tell them; they have forsaken My law, which I set before them, and have not listened to and obeyed My voice nor have they walked in accordance with it" (Jeremiah 9:13), and that it is "your own wickedness [that] shall chasten and correct you, and your backslidings and desertion of faith shall reprove you. [Because] you have forsaken the Lord your God . . ." (Jeremiah 2:19). "You have rejected and forsaken Me. You keep going in reverse, therefore I will stretch out My hand against you and *destroy you*; I am weary of relenting [concerning *your punishment*]" (Jeremiah 15:6).

The soul that sins will die, not by the hand of the Lord, but by its own sliding away from the protective shield, the Lord's mighty hand—a dreadful choice made by people whose hearts have been seared and callused. Let us, rather, dwell among the righteous!

The People in Repentance and Obedience: Confession of Sins

In the following paragraphs, we will discuss what happens when the people (and this should include all those who believe in Adonai Messiah) hear and understand "If My people that are called by My name shall humble themselves, repent and turn from their wicked ways, and seek My face, then will I hear them, and answer their prayer and heal their land" (2 Chronicles 7:14). The statement encapsulates God's principal expectation of His people. If we repent of our sins and cry out to God for Restoration, the Lord God will Forgive us and Restore us to Himself. He will rebuke our enemies and salvage us.

Emeka Anonyuo, Ph.D.

Admission of Omission and Repentance and Confession

And they said unto me, the remnants that are left of the captivity there in the province are in great affliction and reproach: the wall of Jerusalem also is broken down, and the gates thereof are burned with fire. And it came to pass, when I heard these words, that I sat down and wept, and mourned certain days, and fasted, and prayed before the God of heaven, And said, I beseech thee, O Lord God of heaven, the great and terrible God, that keeps covenant and mercy for them that love him and observe his commandments: Let thine ear now be attentive, and your eyes open, that thou may hear the prayer of thy servant, which I pray before thee now, day and night, for the children of Israel thy servants, and **confess the sins of the children of Israel, which we have sinned against thee: both I and my father's house have sinned. We have dealt very corruptly against thee, and have not kept the commandments, nor the statutes, nor the judgments, which thou commandedst thy servant Moses.** (Nehemiah 1. 3-7)

Let us hearken with our hearts to the secret doorway back into the presence of the Lord after one has strayed:

Now in the twenty and fourth day of this month the children of Israel were assembled with fasting, and with sackcloth, and earth upon them. And the seed of Israel separated themselves from all strangers, and stood and confessed their sins, and the iniquities of their fathers. And they stood up . . . and read in the book of the law of the Lord their God *one* fourth part of the day; and *another* fourth part they confessed, and worshipped the Lord their God. After they had fasted, prayed and read from the Book of the Law for hours, even days, Jeshua said, "Stand up *and* bless the Lord your God for ever and ever: and blessed be thy glorious name, which is exalted above all blessing and praise." (Nehemiah 9:1-5)

When Israel realized their stubbornness, they cried out, "Now, O our God, what can we say after this? For we have forsaken Your commands?" (Ezra 9:10;). A student of the Torah will wonder, "But Israel rebelled against the Lord a multitude of times; were they hard of hearing or insensitive to the very presence that pervaded and protected them at all times?" And the answer will be, "But they repented of their sins in the same fashion those many times." It is not advisable to sin because we are aware and depend on the abundance of God's Grace. But the fact is that, whenever we are overtaken by sin, we can seek Forgiveness. Just as the wisdom of God counseled the Israelites, it counsels us today. Let us repent and confess offences so that Forgiveness can ensue!

It is easy to discern a pattern of sin and Forgiveness, as we find in a tapestry or mosaic. For each time when they had learnt their lessons the hard way, "they cried to the Lord, saying, 'we have sinned because we have forsaken the Lord and have served the Baals and the Ashtaroth; but now deliver us from the hands of our enemies, and we will serve You'" (1 Samuel 12:10).

That was the proposal that Adonai was waiting to hear, one devoid of haughtiness and self-righteous justifications and rationalizations. Brethren, that was not for the Israelites alone; the same goes for all who believe in Adonai Yeshua.

See, they have quit pretending or making excuses. They did not try to fault or blame God as they had done in the days of their ignorance—as some of us still do. They humbly confessed their sins and threw themselves on the Mercy of the One and Only True Judge, Yahweh Elohim.

> O Lord, the Hope of Israel, all who forsake You shall be put to shame. They who depart from You and me [Your prophet] shall [disappear like] writing upon the ground, because they have forsaken the Lord, the Fountain of living waters. (Jeremiah 17:13)

Visualizing The Day of Repentance

> And all the people gathered themselves together as one man into the street that *was* before the water gate; and they spake unto Ezra the scribe

to bring the book of the Law of Moses, which the
LORD had commanded to Israel. And Ezra the
priest brought the law before the congregation
both of men and women, and all that *could hear
with understanding*,

And he read therein . . . from the morning until
midday . . . and the ears of all the people *were
attentive* unto the book of the law. And Ezra the
scribe stood upon a pulpit of wood, which they had
made for the purpose . . . and opened the book in
the sight of all the people . . . and when he opened
it, all the people stood up.

And Ezra blessed the Lord, the great God.
And all the people answered, Amen, Amen, with
lifting up their hands: and they bowed their heads,
and worshipped the Lord with *their* faces to the
ground. (Nehemiah 8:1-5)

Let us pause for a moment and see if we can understand
what was going on. "Ezra read the Book from the morning
until midday . . . And Ezra blessed the Lord, the great God.
And all the people answered, Amen, Amen, with lifting up
their hands: and they bowed their heads, and worshipped the
Lord with *their* faces to the ground." Is that what happens
today in our churches, temples, and synagogues? Can you
see the problem? What has become *our* pulpit, *our* church,
our service, etcetera used to be Adonai's. After all, He never
ceases to be Yahweh Shammah, the Lord Who Is Always

Here. To fully understand where He is these days, if not in the Temple, ask Ezekiel what (Ezekiel 10:1) happened after the Lord showed the Prophet the abominations that the Elders were committing in the sanctuary of the Lord. What happened? The Spirit of the Lord left the temple, which is to say that the congregants and temple leaders forsook the Lord, separated themselves from Him.

Please check your place of worship and make certain that Adonai still inhabits the praises of the congregation. If not, separate yourself from them. Do not worry about being called a Church, synagogue or temple hopper.

Comprehending His Voice Makes all the Difference

Continuing with their confessions, repentance, and contrition, Jeshua and the Levites caused the people to understand the law. So they read in the book the law of God distinctly and gave the sense and caused *them* to understand the reading.

"Nehemiah, which *is* the Tirshatha, and Ezra the priest, the scribe, and the Levites that taught the people, said unto all the people, This day *is* holy unto the LORD your God; mourn not, nor weep. For all the people wept, when they heard the words of the law" (Nehemiah 8: 1-8).

That is exactly what happens, and should happen, when the Holy Spirit ordains and guides leaders committed to their calling "to pasture the people of God."

Experiencing That Day of Confession

Let us picture what must have happened on that day of confession—possibly reminiscent of King Solomon's dedication of the Tabernacle—the huge gathering of the people, leaders and the led, all. There were exuberant chanting, choruses, and blasts of the *shofar*, trumpets, and other instruments commonly featured each time the people gathered honestly and humbly to supplicate Adonai and celebrate His goodness. They prostrated themselves as their leaders gestured in the same position. The Israelites cried to the Lord in unison, saying, *"*Forgive O Adonai . . . for we have sinned against You, because we have forsaken our God and have served the Baals*"* (Judges 10:10). A determined listener can still hear chants from the ancient choir, praising and supplicating the Ancient of Days: "Lord have mercy, Lord have mercy, for we have placed all our hopes in You."

Even though they did not have to, they did vindicate God, accepting the blame and admitting that the evil had befallen them because "[they] [had] forsaken [their] God [not the other way]" as the accusers of God, the fault finders, have done and continue to do.

It would be after the confessions, conviction, and restoration that the Israelites would have to have said, "But as for us, the Lord is our God, and we have not forsaken Him. We have priests ministering to the Lord who are sons of Aaron, and Levites for their service" (2 Chronicles 13:10).

More on the People's Confessions and the Vindication of God

> For we are bondmen; yet our God has not forsaken us in our bondage, but has extended mercy and steadfast love to us before the kings of Persia, to give us some reviving to set up the house of our God, to repair its ruins, and to give us a wall [of protection] in Judah and Jerusalem. (Ezra 9:9)

When the spiritual blindness was healed, the people were able to see the true image of their Heavenly Father in a way they never had before. As their knowledge of Him grew, so did their confidence in and reliance upon Him. It was in this state of bliss that the Psalmist wrote, "And they who know Your name [who have experience and acquaintance with Your mercy] will lean on and confidently put their trust in You, for You, Lord, have not forsaken those who seek You [on the authority of God's Word and the right of their necessity] (Psalm 9:10; 42:1).

God's Reaction after the People's Confession

After the people's repentance, confession and contrition, Adonai, the Blessed One, answered from His holy mountain, "And I will bring the blind by a way that they know not; I will lead them in paths that they have not known. I will make darkness into light before them and make uneven places into a plain. These things I have determined to do [for them]; and I will not leave them forsaken" (Isaiah 42:16). Are you tapping into all of these for yourself?

The Faithfulness of our Lord, His Love, Mercy, and Grace came flowing like a torrent of many waters as He reassured them: "Whereas you have been forsaken and hated, so that no man passed through you, I will make you [Jerusalem] an eternal glory, a joy from age to age" (Isaiah 60:15).

Adonai's excitement and enthusiasm are vividly portrayed by the promises that He made:

> You [Judah] shall no more be termed Forsaken, nor shall your land be called Desolate any more. But you shall be called Hephzibah [My delight is in her], and your land be called Beulah [married]; for the Lord delights in you, and your land shall be married [owned and protected by the Lord]. (Isaiah 62:4)

And they shall call them the Holy People, the
Redeemed of the Lord; and you shall be called
Sought Out, a City Not Forsaken. (Isaiah 62:12)

The Book of Lamentations

The Book of Lamentations is, in fact, Prophet
Jeremiah's admission that the Lord let the people suffer the
consequences of their rebelliousness.

A study, even peripherally, of the Holy Scriptures,
especially the writings of the Prophets, shows a repetitive
pattern of God's promises to safeguard Israel, the people's
constant rebellion against God's Commandments, the
resultant afflictions, and the flow of God's Unbounded Mercy
and Grace. Considering the innumerable times that Adonai
threatened Israel but spared them, an uninspired student,
lacking in discernment, might think that God does not quite
make up His mind. However, it is this enduring pattern of
God's Mercy and Grace that grants hope to every man and
woman. No matter how crimson our sins are, Adonai, the
impartial One, will honor His promise and His perfect Lamb
Jesus Messiah. He Will Wash us white as snow.

To receive maximum benefits from Adonai, offenders
must fulfill the conditions stipulated: turn away from
their rebellion, confess their sins, ask for Forgiveness
and Restoration, seriously make an act of contrition,
and, when possible, make restitution. After all, Adonai,

who said that "The heart is deceitful . . . and desperately wicked," and "Cursed be the man who does not keep the Commandments," also promised, "If you walk before Me and be perfect/blameless, I shall bless you" (Genesis 17:1).

We must learn to ask from God whatever we must at our hour of need, and patiently wait for a response at God's Own Pace. Remember that two decades or more after God's promise to Abraham, despite the initial doubts of the would-be beneficiaries, God the Benefactor, being the Epitome of Faithfulness, fulfilled the promise He made: "At a time appointed, I shall return to you" (Genesis 18:14), and He did. The promised seed was Isaac, then you and me.

"I Will Never Forsake You," Said the Lord

There are so many direct and implied references to God Almighty's reiterating His desire and Omniscient, Omnipotent Word, which He exalted above His Name, never to abandon or renounce the righteous. Even a haphazard and marginal study of the Personality of God is enough to pinpoint the dangers inherent in the misunderstanding, misconception, and misinterpretation resulting in the misrepresentation of Adonai. Let us be careful how we understand; may the Holy Spirit alone bring us into all Truth.

Self Destructive Behaviors by Christians

Misunderstandings, misconceptions, and misinterpretations empower many contemporary Christians as well as sworn enemies of Christ to denigrate Adonai and those who believe in Him purely. Building on the shoddy foundations that ignorant Christians have built, haters of the Godhead pretend to have found sufficient reasons to deny, or at least question, Adonai's Omniscience, Omnipotence, Omnipresence, and other Qualities. Those who do not know God but are somehow being drawn by His Spirit sit on the sidelines, getting negative signals from Christians as to who Adonai really Is.

This state of chaos exists because halfhearted, untaught Christians, who "perish for lack of understanding," have contradicted themselves, critiqued and hypercriticized the Holy Bible, accused God, indicted God, and convicted God of being nonexistent or of lacking the Omniness ascribed to Him, flip-flopping on His promises. No other religious group of people is so potently poisonous to its own survival as the contemporary Christian Church.

Disconnecting the *New Testament* From the *Old*: What Has the Contemporary Christian Gleaned From The Experiences of The Israelites?

One would think the experiences of Israel with Adonai would have served to advise contemporary Christians as to who Yahweh Adonai really is, how He can be known, what His requirements of His children are, and what His reactions are when His Laws are not obeyed. No, 21st-century Christians consider themselves the new Israelites: abandoned. They believe the devil-inspired displacement theology asserting that Adonai has abandoned the original Israel because of her non-acceptance of Messiah Yeshua. What misguided thinking! I will not use this precious time and space to discuss the likes of displacement theology and its anti-semitic proponents. Can we love the mango fruit but hate the tree? Can we ask for Abraham's blessings, receive the Forgiveness and Blessings of Yeshua Messiah, and, at the same time, hate His brothers and sisters? God exhorts us, "If you do this for the least of my brethren, you have done it unto me" (Matthew 25:40). "I will bless those who bless you but curse those who hate you" (Genesis 12:3).

What the Accusers of the Brethren See When they Look at the Contemporary Christian

We have seen that the most egregious accusation brought against God is that, after He promised not to forsake His children, the righteous, He has consistently done so.

Adonai Yeshua and His believing followers hear the voices of the accusers singing in unison that, if God were Almighty, surely He would have Foreknown that the multitude of man's sins would cause Him to forsake His Son. If God Foreknew His renunciation of His only begotten Son, when Jesus most needed His Father's love, surely God would have Foreknown not to claim He would never forsake mankind. Are the accusers right? Did God forsake Christ because Adonai was not appropriately equipped to handle the so-called magnitude of sins that were to flood Jesus at Calvary? Was the Almighty and eternal Father of the universe taken unawares? See the power of ignorance!

A Melody That God Wrote

The Truth that God Formed us in His own image, after His likeness; that sin, through the ministry of Satan, deforms us; and that God, through Christ, Redeems and Transforms us is a melody Written by God long before Adam and Eve. This Truth—because it is the Truth—bears repetition.

God—the Infinite One, Alpha and Omega, Author of all things—Foreknew that mankind was going to blow the chance for everlasting bliss in the Garden. Even then, for reasons the Holy Scriptures impress upon us, Adonai readied Himself to "step down from heavenly glory and dwell among men" (Luke 1:5-8), cleanse mankind from the offenses we had committed, and show us that the right way to live is to die to sin, sow to the Spirit, and harvest Eternal Bliss. Believing the truth of this statement prepares us to understand why Christ came, what He did, and what He accomplished through His crucifixion, but especially by His Resurrection. It also helps us to comprehend correctly what Christ actually said on the cross when He cried out, "Eloi, Eloi, Lama sabacthani [My God, My God, why have you forsaken Me]?"

Let us not join the pandemic chorus of disembodied voices chanting the cacophonous refrain "God Forsook Jesus and forsakes us, too!" "God forsook Jesus and forsakes us, too!" "God forsook Jesus and forsakes us, too!"

And Adonai Exclaimed, "Oops"

What has been implied by such teachings about God's abandonment of Christ is that when the Almighty God was overwhelmed and traumatized by how much He did not know, upon seeing the multitude of sins on His dying Son, Adonai whimpered, "Oops! I underestimated the size of mankind's errors. I wasn't quite ready to deal with sins of such magnitude and complexity. I guess I'll just have to turn away, eat my words, and forsake my Son. Oh, well. Better luck next time."

Anyone voicing such balderdash—such widespread claptrap that God the Father abandoned His Son, the Spotless Sacrificial Lamb Who Is Also God—Is saying that God is not Almighty or Omniscient. Is He? Or is He not? We must take care in how we answer, because our response is a choice that will determine our final resting place—hell or Heaven!

Emeka Anonyuo, Ph.D.

Forsaken: the Job Factor

Considering all human suffering, Job's anguish epitomizes torment—physical, psychological, and emotional. It is the worst-case scenario of invasion by dark forces. By all accounts, he was a righteous man. Yet everyone who knew him was certain he had done something really ugly, or else God would not have forsaken him. Previously, to human eyes, he was a benevolent man, a benefactor to many. More importantly, before God, Job was also a righteous man, one who did what was pleasing to the Lord. How, then, did a man who enjoyed the superlative respect of men and women, boys and girls, one who was declared righteous by the Supreme Judge of the universe, come to such a harrowing existence?

What did Job think about his plight? Whom did he accuse of doing this to him? He said, "Even though you slay me, yet will I put my trust in you" (Job 13:15). Who was he talking to? Was he right about his accusation? Was God responsible for Job's sufferings? Though the victim seemed to believe that God was responsible, was He? Did God ever forsake Job anytime through his ordeal? Even after every one of his friends had accused Job of varied forms of sins and abandoned him? Even after Job's sweetheart advised that Adonai be cursed? Is it possible that Job heard directly from God that "the righteous will never be forsaken"?

The story of Job is believed to be the older of the first testaments to the Love of God for His children and especially God's Promise to His children that those who put their trust in Him will not die, be disappointed, or be forsaken. His chronicle began with a "bet" between God Almighty and Satan. The devil, who always envied the Sovereignty, the Supremacy, of God, decided to discredit Him before His children by attacking one of those considered to be a true exhibiter of God's goodness. The Omniscient God, not willing to allow any form of contest with Satan and Foreknowing the devil's intention, directed the tempter to one of God's children who would be more than a match for the antagonist.

Adonai asked, "Have you considered my servant Job?" The adversary said yes but quickly added accusingly that the reason Job could not be touched was because Adonai had put a hedge around the man. "Take down the hedge, and Job is dead meat," thought Satan. We know the rest of the dialogue leading to Satan's commissioning himself to destroy the relationship between God and His creation. The adversary hoped to accomplish his evil intent by planting doubts in the minds of God's children and birthing suspicions that God is not Omnipotent, Omniscient, or Trustworthy.

We must always be mindful that no one is insulated from the accusations and temptations of our wily cosmic adversary. Job's story epitomizes our vulnerability. But it also epitomizes the Truth about Faith and about God. When God challenged Satan to try to break Job, Adonai Foreknew that, although Job would suffer horrifically, he would not break. He would appear to be breaking, and he would even fear he was breaking. But through his terrible agony he would sustain his Faith in God. Although many times Job did *feel* as if God had abandoned him, he continued to *proclaim* that God was his Steadfast Refuge and Salvation, no matter what.

Hence, Yahweh Elohim never left Job's "side." Not for a moment. God is Always Present. But we do not sense His Presence and know that He Is Present unless we have pure Faith in Him, as Job did. It was Job's Faith that sustained him when nothing of worth was left for him, with him, or in him. But for the Presence within Job of the Glorious One of Israel, the man would have been food for the spiritual vultures. Satan tempted and tormented him brutally, but was beaten. Adonai proved to the enemy of our souls that He, Adonai, owns us and will continue to sustain those of us who have true Faith and, with diligence, believe in and follow Him.

God Perfected Job in the Crucible of Fiery Trials

God cannot tempt and cannot be tempted. (This boldly questions the accuracy of the spectacle entitled "The Temptations of Christ" and its fashionable interpretations.) However, Adonai uses temptations, trials, and testing as tools. It can be said that God "perfected" Job through this mind-bending ordeal (see Job: 42. 1-6). Listen to Job speak to Yahweh Adonai after the unprecedented marathon nightmare: "I know that you can do all things, no plan of yours can be thwarted. Surely, I spoke of things I did not understand, things too wonderful for me to know. My ears had heard of you, but now, my eyes have seen you. Therefore I despise myself and repent in dust and ashes".

The Lesson That Job Learnt: a Model for Today's Believers in Adonai-Yeshua

Many life lessons are laid bare here. But what is most clearly projected is this: Job had thought that he knew God well (as most of us do) but discovered that he did not—only because of his many tests, trials, and tribulations. Pay attention and hear his convincing testimony: "My ears had heard of you, but now my eyes have seen you." Paraphrased, it would read like this: "I thought I knew you, I did not, but now, after my ordeal, I do. Forgive my presumptions, O Lord." Shouldn't we be supplicating the same way, even louder?

Adonai Was Within Job All Along, As He Is With Us Right Now

If Adonai had forsaken Job, the man would not have made it through the nerve-busting, mind-bending, faith-draining ordeal bordering on the macabre and horrific. If Adonai had not been right beside him all the time, Job's eye would not have "seen" Him. Job "saw" Adonai because He was there all the time, as Jehovah Shammah, Immanuel, the Omnipresent God, is Always with us. Hence "My eyes have seen you." We have determined with absolute certainty that the Omnipotent One did not forsake Job, David, the Israelites, His only begotten Son, or anyone else. Nor will He ever forsake you and me—If we remain corrigible and continually aspire to righteousness.

Emeka Anonyuo, Ph.D.

Where the Accusation Against God's Constancy and Omniness Began and How It Is Sustained

If it is true that God does not forsake, has never forsaken, and will never forsake the righteous, then where did this whole accusation that He does stem from? Why and how has this blasphemous thought gained strength and been disseminated? Why has it persisted in Christian theology? And how have men and women who are aware of the profusion of testimonies to God's Steadfast Omniness found Him guilty of desertion and, therefore, labeled Him an equivocator?

The answer to those questions can be summarized in one word: ignorance. "My people die for lack of knowledge" (Hosea 3). The Speaker was not talking about lack of seminary or university education. He was actually addressing the frightening deviation from the Whole Word of Truth in favor of fables and goose bumps authored by Satan. Adonai was calling our attention to the out-of-sequence aspiration to demystify His existence without "fear of the Lord," when, in actuality, fear of God is the beginning of wisdom. But, alas, godly wisdom and knowledge have been exchanged for the "wisdom of the ages," as propounded by the classical sages, mere fallible men, some of whom represented the epitome of depravity and profanity.

Mortar-and-brick university seminaries, where professors teach theology sprinkled with classical humanism and modern, secular humanism have replaced the "wilderness school" attended by many prophets and apostles, including Saint John the Baptizer. The Torah teaches about God, the Koran talks about Allah, Buddhists clamor after the Buddha, and the Hindi submit to the pantheon of their gods. But of all religious literature, both the revealed and man-made, the Holy Bible seems to be the only compilation that has suffered most at the hands of those for whom it was written. The situation reminds me of a man who has been provided a tent to shelter him from the winter's cold but who would rather stand over a fire holding a water hose to douse the flame generated to keep him warm.

Christians are the only people who have consciously rebelled against their God, Father Adonai, and His Word. Too much studying has pushed us to the brinks of insanity. In seeking more than godly knowledge and wisdom, we have gathered both wheat and chaff into the barn with no winnowing in mind. Christians, though not so many true believer-followers of "the Way," have most readily corrupted Adonai's inerrant Word with Greco-Roman mythology and its gods and goddesses. What has crystallized from this hybridization is something like a rainbow culture. Although devoid of substance, it very much appeals to the romantic fancy of contemporary Christianity.

Mankind's initial honest aspiration was to find the God of the Torah, but somewhere during the journey, we met the modernist and postmodernist philosopher-theologians and were consumed by the new thoughts that seek to "modernize" God, stripping Him of His Unfathomable, Immutable *Ancientness*.

Contemporary Christians and their modernist views and teachings have drastically distanced themselves from the authentic traditional teachings of the Venerable Master, Yeshua the Messiah. What has happened is that the secular-humanist churches, now immersed in and overpowered by the allure of flamboyant, lustful desires, have garnered unto themselves a followership that looks up to them for spiritual nourishment. Each man and each woman, being right in his or her own eyes, has arrogated the unique attribute of Adonai's *Omniscience*. They have all the answers; and even more disturbing, they have the means of making the spiritually hungry but stupefied congregants ingest and believe their half-baked spiritual cuisine. The blind preacher now leads a throng of blind people, and we do not need prophets to tell us what the outcome of this blasphemy will be. An ominous beginning—a horrific end!

The Amputation of the Word of God

To support their new profane theology, these egotistical theologians scour the Holy Scriptures, the Lord's Holy Word, written down by anointed writers, with a mind to editing out Commandments and Precepts that are too hard to accept. In their places, these Word censors have the gall to create their own diluted version, more mundane but, not surprisingly, more desirable for faltering contemporary micro-wave Christians.

Mankind's determination to dismantle and humanize God has gained speed. The deification of mere humans is near completion. The new gospel according to the fantasy of the new prophet-pastor-apostle-music director-founder-CEO, all in one, takes precedence over the Holy Bible. After such excision and revision, what remains is a collection of mere fables. Ever thought about the difference between the Bible and the Holy Bible? The teachings of the Hollywood superstar wannabe pastor are published, audio-recorded, filmed, and distributed—"highly recommended" for congregants who "genuinely" seek entrance to heaven. Where is that? A spa in Los Angeles?

What truly wrenches the heart is the sight of unsuspecting knowledge-seeking brethren who collect the adulterated "word of God" with feverish religious zeal. Sweet words, laced with spiritual intoxicants, presented in a potion of missionary mumbo jumbo and Shakespearean oratory, intimidate innocent congregants into believing that evil is good. I wish we still had Bereans among contemporary Christians, courageous people who would ask hard questions, fact check what they have heard against the Word of God, and refuse to be swayed if they are not filled by the Holy Spirit. As the accursed concoction replaces the demanding truth of the Holy Bible, Heaven frowns, while hell celebrates, and the credulous congregants throw themselves in and swim with exhilaration in this monstrous cesspool of putrefaction called secular humanist Christianity.

Beware what you listen to, what you read, and what you believe because the making of books has proliferated the mischievous doctrines designed to derail the true seekers of Yeshua. Heed the warning of God and His anointed servants. (Read "The Making of Too Many Books" in "Appendices.") Yes, learn from those Nicolaitans, whose carnality and insatiable desire to satisfy flesh drove them onto a collision course with the Word and Will of God the Almighty.

Chapter 4

THE PROLOGUE TO THE EPILOGUE

Pulling It All Together in the Person of the Venerable Jesus Messiah: Adonai's Portrait

The rhythmic nature of the major theme of this book was not designed to bore or frustrate but to emphasize the faith-building Truth, which is that the Almighty God does not forsake any of His obedient children and that those who feel forsaken are actually not forsaken by God but are the ones who are forsaking Adonai by losing Faith and committing unrighteous acts. Such people are encouraged to stop their rebellion, confess their wrongdoing to Adonai, and reiterate their faith and belief in Yeshua Messiah, the Savior of the world. This way, the Way of Truth, Salvation will be extended to them. You and I are not alone in this fallen state. For the Holy Bible declares that all men and women have sinned and therefore fall short of the Glory of Adonai. AND it declares that when we confess our sins, Adonai, being Faithful, Fair, and Just, surely restores us to Divine Fellowship with Him. We are remade anew—ever mindful of our ongoing challenge to live godly lives in His Keeping, ever mindful that new wine cannot be stored in an old wine skin.

Emeka Anonyuo, Ph.D.

The Foundation of Salvation Has No Accommodation for Divine Isolation

Salvation's foundation was laid before Genesis but began from Genesis with the Fall of mankind. Since this is the case, it then means that the Almighty Foreknew that Adam and Eve were going to be tempted by the cunningly and exceedingly intelligent "serpent," that they would make the wrong decision and choose the taste and temporary satisfaction of the fruit over the expectation of Eternal Fellowship with Him. Even though the Almighty warned them against the separation that would occur and the chasm that would exist between them if they ate the forbidden fruit, the Creator put in place a Perfect Salvation Plan.

Adonai Likened to an Expectant Mother

Adonai was not taken unawares by the original sin or any other sins. Not at all. The pregnant mother prepares for the birth and nurturing of her newborn before it is born. She, among many anticipated needs, acquires diapers. She *knows* the child will do the things that come naturally. Her maternal instincts and actions are human versions of certain Divine Qualities of our Heavenly Father. Because Adonai is Omniscient, He already Knew that man was going to *fall*, disobey, and rebel against His instructions. Adonai does not retrospect and, therefore, does not repent as humankind does. The Omniscient One, because of His Immeasurable Loving Kindness, Knowing that He could not and would not leave mankind separated from Him, made an Inflexible Provision for Atonement and Restoration. Hence *Yom Kippur*.

The Holy One would need a Perfect Redeemer to bring mankind back to Him, a Redeemer who would look like the fallen one but who would be filled with the Substance of *El Shaddai*, the Holy Spirit. It can be said simply that Adonai wanted to show Satan that He, God, had the power and resources to equip mankind against the enemy of our souls, so that we will not always be his victims. When the Lord is with us, we have no reason to fear people or spirits. The battle is His, not ours. All we need do is stand still, praise, worship, and adore Him, then witness and accept our salvation. That is what He Promised, and His Word is Truth.

Before Adonai deployed His original plan of Redemption, He had graciously given mankind opportunities to present one of our kind—after the near extinction of forests and domesticated beasts used for sacrifice—one of our kind who was righteous, good, and blameless. But none existed. Prophets came and went. Priests, rulers, judges, and kings emerged and withered, going the way of all flesh. But none was found spotless to become the Atonement. This was because all men and women had sinned and fallen short of the glory of God. Of course, there was One destined to come according to the proclamations of prophets, One who would be Blameless and, therefore, serve as the Perfect Lamb that would take away the *sin* of the world. For that purpose, He would be born Immanuel, "God with us."

Adonai's Original Intent: Yeshua, Our Messiah, Was Not an Option

Christ was not an option. His mission on earth was born with the very first "Thought" in the mind of the Almighty, who is at once the Father, the Son and the Holy Spirit. The Gospel writer John opened his book thus: "In the beginning was the Word and the Word was with God, and the Word was God, and the Word was made flesh and dwelt among men." And the Book of Revelations speaks of the One who sits on the Throne and the One whose Name is the Word of God. Glory, Honor, Power, Worship, and Excellency belong to our God, Adonai Yeshua.

Why was the Word made flesh? Why did God not just expunge mankind by speaking to his frailty or rebuking the deceiver? Why did the Venerable Christ have to come and be "encased" in human flesh? We believe that He came not merely to Redeem mankind and Reconcile mankind to God but that, by coming in the "flesh," He intended to, and did, Model Righteousness, without which no man or woman could ever see God. He came to teach us how to walk through life in the physical world with all its snares, trials, and tribulations, without fainting, without offending our Maker.

The most important questions of all, which I would like to discuss further, are Why was Christ "born," and why did He have to "borrow" the perishable and corruptible human cloak to dwell among us?

Why the Venerable Jesus Was Born?

Many true Christians, real believers in and followers of Yeshua, know *why* the Blessed One was born. This is not the case with non-Christians and nominal Christians, whose major issue is usually *when* He was born. They generally believe He was born on Christmas Day, in a season to be jolly, a season to give and receive gifts in celebration of the birth anniversary of this "unknown God." This unknown is filled with their fantasies and imaginings. Conversely, the believer-followers of the Venerable Yeshua know that the Truth is not about confirming the birth date of Christ, but about understanding the reason for His coming and the significance of His life "in the flesh," His ministry, His death, and His Resurrection. What separates Him from the best of the rest of us is the Redemptive Work He did at Calvary, the impossible-to-duplicate Sacrifice He made for the whole of mankind. With Him, because of Him, "It is finished."

Reasons abound as to why the Infinite seemingly became "finite." They vary among innumerable Christian organizations and denominations, theological schools, and philosophical systems. It would be fair to suggest that these many variations within the Christian faiths are born by the genuine desire and zeal to understand the Holy Trinity, Christ, Christianity, and Christians. These efforts have led to some truly enlightening, spirit-inspired discourses. But most are heterogeneous intellectualizations and bastardizations of the Word—of the Mind of Adonai. They expose humanity to dangerous thinking of tsunami proportions, including influences from the classical pagan cultures of ancient Greece and Rome, which are now being replicated by modern societies of the world.

Perhaps the most frighteningly infectious thinking comes from secular-humanist-infested seminaries. They engender secular-liberal Christianity, no doubt with good intentions, but their fashionable theology overflows with rebellious misinterpretations of the Word of Adonai. Dressed in costumes of righteousness and truth, these insidious microorganisms spread within our churches, slowly but surely infecting the core culture of traditional Christianity. Brothers and sisters, as true *traditional* Christians, we hold Christ as our Center; we are filled and inspired by the Holy Spirit; we are sustained by absolute belief in God, righteous fear of God, and pure love of God. We believe in His Word, and we reject all false claims about His Word.

Let us explore further the key issue, which goes beyond the simple question of why Christ was born. Let us consider why the Word that existed before the creation of mankind and the entire universe was *made flesh* to *"dwell among us."* Our assumption is that most of those who would be interested in this book, and would, hopefully, read it, would be those who know that Jesus Christ, the Messiah-Redeemer, came down to earth "in the flesh" to be the Propitiation for the *sin* of mankind, to bring God back to us, and, through His crucifixion, death, and Resurrection, bring us back to God. Or, as John Milton wrote in *Il Penseroso,* summarizing Italian Baroque (Counter-Reformation) art, to "bring all heavens before [our] eyes." Although Jesus was "tested and tempted in every possible way," He emerged unscathed, without sin or blemish. As a result of His singular Uniqueness, He became the only True, Perfect, Exemplary Model for mankind to follow—if we are interested in a virtuous, godly, victorious life. Yeshua's life simply says that we can live a clean and godly life in spite of the multitude of stumbling blocks on our life's journey.

Christ Insisted That His Apostles Do More Than Listen. He Instructed Them to Watch Him. Why?

Our Master taught His apostles and other disciples, to not only listen to Him intently, but also to watch Him very closely. A good coach elicits both visual and aural attentiveness from his or her players. A good teacher of art or music elicits the same from his or her students. We normally associate music with hearing, and yet some who are deaf play instruments. An accomplished violinist, Jiji Fong, an acquaintance in college, once said, "The blind are sighted; they see through their fingers, and the deaf, their ears have eyes." The apostles did not have visual or aural deficiencies, but did exhibit some degree of spiritual dwarfism—the reason why the Messiah commanded them to watch and listen to Him intently.

Emeka Anonyuo, Ph.D.

Lecture at the Garden of Gethsemane

Why did Christ insist that His apostles both watch and listen? Because He wished them to do, not merely what He said, but also as He did—unlike most religious leaders of our time. He wanted them to observe exactly how He dealt with life's issues from moment to moment and to incorporate their observations into their own daily lives. For example, when Christ went up to pray at the Garden of Gethsemane, He took three of them along and required them to join in the supplication. When the apostles fell asleep, He woke them to be witnesses to the heavenly visitation. They were going to see the mighty One humble Himself, kneel on the dirt, hands and face raised to the skies in supplication. They were going to be witnesses to the acceptability of showing fear in the face of great trial and the necessity of trusting the Power of God to Save. They were going to be taught by the Master Himself to surrender to God in times of good and in times of tribulation. Yes, they would see their Master, the Exalted One, cry out between sobs, "Let this cup pass me by, but if not, may your will be done." He was going to teach them to know beyond words and miracles that God's Will can be trusted because His entire Intention for us is Always Good. That's why He insisted they watch and pray and watch.

A Perfect Model

One of the greatest lessons that we can learn from the earthly sojourn of Adonai in human flesh is that Christ was not, is not, will not be merely the Perfect Lamb. As well, He is *the* Exemplary Model for mankind to emulate. Evangelist Christophe Gregoire, in his sermon titled "Reverence and the Venerable," poignantly illustrated one of the more fundamental lessons that Christ taught us all at the Garden during His Passion. Christophe pointed to the posture that the Master assumed at prayer. "He knelt down [may have fallen to His knees] on the garden dirt and, with His bare knuckles, may have, in agony, pounded the rocky surface of the 'podium' that bore His tottering and emaciated body weight, what was left of it. Tears raining down His face must have mixed with blood being squeezed out from distended, overburdened, and now hemorrhaging blood capillaries, even before Calvary."

The apostles saw it all. They knew that they needed to look, behold, and document all that earthly and heavenly drama unfolding before their eyes, because their Master designed it so. The Word that was made flesh did not only share the Word of Truth with His disciples, but He also demonstrated the Word of Truth at work in the flesh.

When Adonai promised not to forsake His people, He fashioned what we might describe as "uni-relay occupation of the earth." He worked through prophets, priests, and kings in the days of the Torah; came down to earth in the form of man, working as Jesus Messiah; and, upon the "departure" of Jesus, "sent" the Holy Ghost to dwell among us forever and ever—infusing every sub-atomic particle in creation with His Divine Spirit. Yahweh Shamma and Immanuel are one and the same. With us always is Adonai. That was the promise He made when He said, "I will never forsake you . . . I will be with you even till the end of the age."

Yeshua's Methodology: Why the Demonstrations?

Yeshua Messiah encouraged His listening watchers, His apostles and other disciples, to behold the way to victorious existence on earth, with all its trials and temptations, to behold how He dealt with adversity. Implicitly, the Messiah empowered the apostles and other disciples to understand His mission on earth, so that they could teach their contemporaries and future generations of believers how to apply the Lord's Methodology in their own times of need.

Let all who have ears hear this: A legacy was passed, a baton, a torch, to all future generations. How? By the "silent sermon" of Jesus Christ, the Lord of our lives, the Perfect Exemplar of godly living. That's why He insisted they watch and pray and watch. As well, let us do so with all our hearts!

PowerPoint Presentations: Yeshua's Tools

Why is it so hard for us to embrace *the* principal instructional tool that our Lord Jesus Christ placed foremost: action? "Watch and pray that you may not fall into temptation." Our All-Knowing Master knew that the constant practice of watching—of watchfulness—of mindfulness—of devout prayer—enables us, in good time, *to see—to actually see and experience*—the visible and invisible *mysteries and miracles of holiness* that surround us, that fill us with the Holy Spirit and bless us, that sustain us through our tribulations as human beings devoted to living godly lives, that empower us in every moment *to act* as true Christians. *To act as true Christians* means, not only to believe in and love the Godhead with all our hearts and to love our relatives, friends and other fellow humans, but to share our abiding belief in and love of Adonai with others and to help all who would be Christians to understand the critical difference between the True Word of God and the insidious false thinking rampant in our world.

Alas, our contemporaries are deliberately and diligently reducing our world and our Lord to mere word bites, video bites, sound bites: tee shirts, bumper stickers, text messages, tweets, blog posts, Facebook "updates"; YouTube clips, video games, "news" clips, PowerPoint lists, "action" films; political slogans, quotes from speeches presented out of context—you name it! The point is to reduce everything to a "picture," a "glimpse," an "image," as in "a picture is worth a thousand words." There is no debating the fact that, generally speaking, we learn more and faster through visual images. The Lord knows it, and He employs them brilliantly. Yes, *holy mysteries and miracles*, on land, on seas, on mountains, in valleys—everywhere—facilitate conversion to and the construction and fortification of faith in Yeshua. His object is clear and direct: to get the people to see the Greatness of the Love, Power, and Faithfulness of God and to encourage and enable us to believe in Him that we may be saved from the approaching cataclysm.

Pedagogy: Christ's Wisdom Mistaken For Cowardice

Do you remember the number of occasions where Christ had to escape, whether by walking through His assailants or by vanishing into thin air? Why would He evade the opportunities to "show off" His limitless power? Why did He dodge or, as some would say, quit? The lesson for the day was wisdom: "Be wise as the serpent, and as humble as the dove." Remember that Messiah had actually instructed His apostles that if they were persecuted in one location, they should leave for another place. To some of us, what Christ did at those times would amount to showing fear and exhibiting faithlessness and powerlessness. Such a thought would have to come from brazen ignorance because "Adonai has not given us the spirit of fear, but of love, power, and sound mind" to discern and act wisely at all times.

Why, then, should God-Incarnate "show fear" for which He had provided an antidote—not a boring anecdote? Would the Master's exhibiting of fear not be a travesty, a contradiction that would cause irreversible damage to the image of God? Remember what happened shortly after all that tearful, agonizing travail in prayer in the Garden of Gethsemane? Those who always look to find causes, upon seeing none because they lack Christian *watchfulness*, manufacture trumped-up reasons to call Christ's reaction in the Garden "cowardice," morbid "fear" of the uncertainty of His future. To them, sadly for us, what a paradox that He who is Omniscient, Knowing the end before the beginning, suddenly went blank and freaked out at the thought of imminent demise!

Another Paradox: Christ Outnumbered and Overpowered?

Let us consider another criminal absurdity: that our All-Powerful Lord was surrounded and outnumbered by robotic Roman soldiers and treacherous Jewish religious leaders. Outnumbered? For lack of a less absurd illustration, can the U.S. Naval Commander and a division of top-dog Seals be overpowered by a mere swarm of ragtag soldiers? It is sometimes said, preached, taught, and written that Christ, if He had so desired, could have called down an infinite number of warring angels to fight for Him. Fight for Him? That is utterly ridiculous, is it not, and we find it hard to believe that anyone with even a basic understanding of the Creator and His creation would dine with the spiritual Lilliputians who preach such messages.

As we have stated numerous times before, Christ did not need to call for assistance. All He needed was to say the word or even think the thought and there would have been a great conflagration of bodies. If an ordinary man had done that, that would have been "cool." Yeshua was no ordinary "man"! He is God! For Him, nothing is impossible! Let us not forget Sodom and Gomorrah, Noah's deluge, or the Tower of Babel. Adonai Yeshua is Always the Same! Anyone interested in a show of power by Jesus Christ is invited to read Apostle John's documentation of what happened when the soldiers came to arrest the Messiah in the Garden. He said, merely, "I am . . ." and the soldiers fell to the ground. Why? Not because our Savior overpowered them as a show of superior physical strength, but because they sensed the Innate Power of His Divine Presence and became overwhelmed. But this book is not about Christ's proving Himself to anyone. It is about finding our way with Him, His Steadfast Promises, and His Completed Work of Redeeming us if we are so committed.

The challenge of understanding the Ineffable Qualities of the Holy Trinity—Inerrancy, Immutability, Infallibility, and All Else Embodied in God's Holy Omniness—is complicated by the secular humanists' efforts to secularize the Word of God and humanize the Divine. In some very disturbing ways, even many Christians have failed to understand the fundamentals of Christianity, viewing God as a man enslaved by his environment. The derisive concept of Christ as "fully God and fully man" seems to have drugged mankind into a slumber state. Contemporary mankind, driven by empiricism and humanism, is able to prove neither that God is God, nor that God is man. Firmly in the clutches of this self-induced confusion, mankind settles for a hybrid concept that mimics Zeus and Apollo as well as the mythological Centaur or Minotaur.

If Jesus Messiah needed an army of men, He would have capitulated to the zealot Barabbas and allowed those who mistook Him for the general-commander-in-chief of the people's army to have crowned Him king. Friends, remember this counsel: "The weapon of our warfare is not carnal but spiritual . . . ." Remember, too, "Sheath your sword, Peter . . . ."

The World is Eroding the Word

Yes, it is eroding the Word as the rivulets of the past become canyons of raging currents. Christians, swept downriver by the forceful Christian adversary, are tossed and pummeled into a state of stupor. Sadly, if understandably, they give in to tolerance of the intolerable and, with ill-founded compromises, accommodate overt pagan hedonistic thinking and practices.

No wonder the blurring of God's True Nature! So many Christians have been so tossed and pummeled that they barely see, hear, or feel. They believe that our heavenly Father, who cannot be tempted, ever, was actually tempted by Satan and had to struggle to keep His hands clear of the cookie jar. That is the ludicrous image of Adonai concocted by the contemporary secular-humanist-liberal Christian church. We strain to comprehend any value whatsoever in the humanizing of the Divine by well-meaning theologians, swept along by the raging current of conventional wisdom. It is popular, yes, but so corrosive of the True Holy Word.

203

Here is a typical example of an honest effort by a believer in, and follower of Yeshua Messiah, singing the popular but erroneous, anthem: "God Himself knew that we would need to be strengthened and encouraged; that's why He became like us and chose to struggle *against the same temptations* that perplex us" (J. Weiss, *God Still Uses Vessels*); (emphasis mine).

Here is another one: "Being made perfect by what He suffered" (Hebrews 5). The statement presupposes that He was not perfect until after the suffering. Where was the "Perfect Lamb of God who would take away the sins of the world" before that? Can/should we literally apply Hebrews 5, Christ's being made perfect by what he suffered, out of context, as we humans are inclined to do? If so, we would be subscribing to the popular, faulty notion that Christ is able to empathize with us in our temptations and sufferings only because He too suffered pain, rejection, and was tempted. Errant nonsense! Let us review that lecture.

Revisiting the "Temptation of Christ"

The story goes that after Christ had fasted for forty days, He became hungry, and the *Holy Spirit* led Him into the wilderness to be tempted by Satan. Tempted? Does not the Holy Bible teach that God does not tempt and cannot be tempted? Don't we pray to God, "Do not lead us into temptation, but deliver us from evil?" Who is equivocating here, the Holy Writ which the true Christian knows to be inerrant or the "Christian" who refuses to be Christ-like? The contemporary Christian somehow believes that He who fed over fifteen thousand (counting women and children) with "five loaves and two fish" was not able to feed Himself. Where or when did Christ ever forego "It is not by bread alone that man lives, but by every word proceeding from the mouth of God"? (Matthew 4:4)

Please do not strain out the flea and swallow the elephant. Yeshua-Adonai was simply modeling—one of the primary reasons why He needed to incarnate and enter the human race. When the apostles asked their Master to "teach us how to pray," they also illustrated the fact that they needed to be taught how to live—precisely what their Omniscient Master did.

Not Moses, Joshua, Elijah, or Any Other Prophet Asked God to Send Angels: Why Should the Messiah? Didactic Leadership

Elijah did not, nor did any other Prophet, ask God to send angels when they were in a quandary. Elijah, literally outnumbered by the priests of Baal, aware of God's Promise and Presence, stayed focused on the mountaintop from whence his help would come. The teenage David did not call for a reinforcement of angels when the man-mountain, the Philistine war machine Goliath, towered over him. Behold One Greater than Elijah and David, the One that Enabled and Sustained them in times of their need. He is here. His name is Yeshua, the Anointed, Venerable One. To Him Be All Power and Majesty! Forever!

Would He ever need angels? No! He was only modeling for the benefit of His apostles. No one with a Direct Line to His Heavenly Father needs angels. Jesus said to those who believed and who would believe in Him, "Call upon me in your hour of need . . .". For reasons not known to any of us, God may sometimes send angels to battle for us. Let us not stray from God. When we call upon Him, Adonai will answer us in His Own Time and in His Own Way.

Would the designer and builder of a sand castle need a special squad of army engineers to level it? Jesus, the Savior of the world, Jesus, the Designer and Builder of the universe, is Self-Sufficient, no matter the task. He is Omnipotent. All Power Belongs to Him, for He Is the Father, the Son, and the Holy Spirit. He cannot be any more—or any less—than He is, for He Is All and Everything! Ineffable! Incomparable!

If Christ Did Not Need Angels, Who Does? Leaving Vital Instructions for His Followers

What message was Christ constantly delivering to His listeners, especially His hearers? First, let us consider this statement: "Don't you know that I can call on my Father and that He would send down millions of Angels to fight for me" (Matthew 26:26).

The lesson is clear: Christ was teaching His disciples to trust God to protect them in times of danger—when they are overwhelmed by the cares of this world or by the wiles of the evil one. Christ said that His believers-followers can do even greater things than He did if they have faith and trust in His Father through Him. Could calling down angels be one of those greater things? No. Indeed that would be a great thing. But why would we request the company of servants when the master of the house has invited us to sit with him at the high banquet table?

Jane Crouch's Vision and Arthur Blessit's Salvation

There are innumerable stories about angels' intervention in human situations. One of the more astounding was narrated by Jane Crouch of the Trinity Broadcasting Network. She told how a vision had revealed to her the harrowing plight of evangelist Arthur Blessit, who was surrounded by a horde of assailants poised to shoot their captive. The TBN matriarch prayed to the Lord for angelic intervention, and indeed a band of invisible angels knocked the assailants to the ground. This event has been verified as accurate.

It is crucial, of course, that we not pray directly to angels but, rather, to God, as sister Crouch did, for praying to angels would be similar to worshipping idols. Some may ask why God did not intervene directly but decided, instead, to send Jane Crouch a vision. That was a form, we might say, of indirect intervention. But who are we to know, or even

Emeka Anonyuo, Ph.D.

question, why or how God does what He does? Nonetheless, the incident has encouraged many Christians to engage in intercessory prayer and significantly boosted the faith of many, including me.

Other important lessons taught by Jesus Messiah include humility and surrendering our will to the Will of God, who alone is the Omniscient Architect of our destiny. Jesus said, "I laid down my life by choice, and if I pleased, I would take it up again" (John 10:18). So when we recall His reprimanding of the zealous Peter, "Sheath your sword Peter; this is the will of my Father," we begin to understand His objective: to show us the pathway to Eternal Bliss with Him and His Father. Believe and trust in Adonai, who is blessed forever!

When we reckon the thoughts behind the statements, we always find a pearl of heavenly wisdom and a harmony among all. Jesus humbled Himself to die, even the shameful death on the cross, and He was led like a sheep to slaughter without raising His voice in protest or proclaiming his innocence. Do we do the same and let God's Will be done?

"I and My Father Are One and the Same," Said Yeshua Messiah. If He is Right, Was He Then Privy to the Plan of Redemption, and if He Was, Why Did He Cry "My God, My God, Why Have You Forsaken Me?"

As a youthful Christian, I thought some evangelists had blasphemed the Lord because they taught that the Son is the same as the Father, the Creator, the Giver and Sustainer of life. It is difficult for some to grasp this Oneness. Actually, we need not grapple with the idea. We simply need take the hand of the Teacher, and He will guide us into all Truth and grant us the knowledge and wisdom to comprehend the Great Mystery.

Listen to what the venerable Yeshua said in the Gospel of John 14:6, 8: "I am the Way, the Truth and the Life . . . if you really knew me, you would know my Father. From now on, you do know Him and have seen Him." Sounding like the doubting Thomas, Philip asked the Master to show them the Father, "and that will be enough for us." And the Lord answered, "Don't you know Me after I have been among you such a long time? Anyone who has seen Me, has seen the Father. Don't you believe that I am in the Father, and the Father in Me? The words that I say to you are not just my own. Rather, it is the Father living in me who is doing His work" (John 16:15). "All that belongs to the Father is mine" (John 16:15).

Listen to this unassuming statement found in John 17:5: "Glorify Me with the glory I had with you before the world began." He is talking about the period before Genesis: "Before Abraham I am," meaning the Word—the Father, the Son, and the Holy Spirit—One Divinity. Also, when the Master prayed for us before His betrayal and death, He asked the Father thus: "Holy Father protect them by the power of thy Name, the name you gave me, so they may be one as we are One.

Protect them by the power of Thy name; the Name you gave to Me" (John 17:11).

The point here is this: if, as Yeshua Messiah said and we ardently believe, He is One with His Father, He must have known of the plan to ransom captive earth and its occupants. He must have known the magnitude of mankind's sin to be able to provide the appropriate cleansing agent. Christ's fervent prayer at Gethsemane unsettles many Christians because Jesus seemed unaware of His Father's Will. Actually, Foreknowing all, for He Himself Is God, He prayed as He did to teach his followers important life lessons. Likewise His widely misunderstood utterance from the cross, "My God my God, why hast thou forsaken me?"

Divine Intentions are spiritually discerned by spiritual people, but to those who are perishing, they seem to be foolishness. If we have enough wisdom to desire the revelation of the Word of God, we simply ask the Lord. He gives freely to all who ask. He is always waiting to equip us with the tools we need to know Him properly. Adonai said, "My people die for lack of understanding." If we know why Jesus Christ came, we also know that Adonai did not forsake His Son on the cross, for we know He never, ever, forsakes the righteous.

What Is God's Name? The Venerable Yeshua HaMachiach. Is That Really It? Let Us Listen Again.

Do we need any more proof to believe what He, Yeshua Messiah, said in explaining who He is? Should we wait for the theologian's endorsement before we can believe Him, or should we not just take Him at His word? Let us not miss the key point here. The principal question and bother of the apostles can be summarized this way: "We have walked with you for these many years and heard great words of wisdom. We have also heard you speak about your Father; we see you physically, but have never seen your Father. Show Him to us, that we may see, and believe [more] completely" (The Vow 2004).

Because of certain limitations, which may include cultural and religious traditions, it has been exceptionally difficult for mankind to believe certain things completely. The Holy Bible is replete with people demanding that God show them a miracle or sign, something for the empirical mind, in order "that we may see before we believe." How much would be enough for the doubting Thomases? The Testaments overflow with impossible miracles and signs, yet the children of God ask for more from Him before they will believe. If it should take only signs and wonders to convince and convert a soul, all Jews, orthodox and Messianic, would have become the leaders—as Adonai, the Blessed One, commissioned them to be—in spreading the Gospel of Yeshua. Even the chosen twelve apostles, who were constantly in the company of the Master, would ask Him to show them the Father.

Problem: so many of us walk by sight and not by faith, yet the Word of God is Spirit and can only be discerned spiritually.

To the request for a physical portrait of Jehovah, the Master's answer was direct, crisp, clear, and unmistakable: "Look at me. [Because the Father and I are one and the same, He in me, I in Him,] I am the Father". Jesus seemed to imply, Any more questions?" (The Vow 2003)

If signs and wonders are all that humans need to believe, the Israelites would have walked straight from Pharaoh's land into the Promised Land without the forty-one-year palaver in the wilderness. But we need more than miracles. We need raw Faith, childlike Faith in God's Word and His Omniness.

Christ the Visible Godhead

> And I will ask the Father to send another Counselor to be with you forever, the Spirit of truth. The world cannot accept Him because it neither sees Him nor knows Him. But you know Him, for He lives with you, and will be in you. I will not leave you as orphans; I will come to you. Before long, the world will not see me anymore, but you will see me . . . . On that day you will realize that I am in my Father, and you are in me, and I am in you. (John 14:16)

Sounds like a riddle. Yes, to those who are perishing and others who are too afraid to step away from the world and wade further into the water—those to whom the writer of the Book of Hebrews posed this question: "How long are we going to continue with the fundamental principles of salvation . . . ?" (6:1) Those would be the ones who do not believe enough and who ask Yeshua for more water from the Fountain of life.

It is depressing to hear people who claim to be "born again" question the correctness of the statement that upholds the existence of the Godhead, some calling it blasphemy. Only those who are not true believers in and followers of the Messiah can cry blasphemy, especially if they have not yet enrolled in the school where the Holy Ghost, Alone, is the Teacher. What has been postulated and explained is very clear: the Father, the Son, and the Holy Spirit are One. Their manifestation on earth was embodied by Yeshua, who is known as Immanuel, the name that He shares with the Father, a name that was given to the Son by the Father. Is Jesus Christ, then, the Holy Spirit? Categorically yes! as in the following scripture:

> And I will ask the Father to send another Counselor to be with you forever, the Spirit of truth. The world cannot accept Him because it neither sees Him nor knows Him. But you know Him, for He lives with you, and will be in you. I will not leave you as orphans; I will come to you. Before

long, the world will not see me anymore, but you
will see me (John 14:15-24).

The act of seeing here communicates the same way as
the "see" in "If you have seen me, you have 'seen' the Father"
or "see" as used in popular culture: Do you "see" what I am
saying? Which of course translates to, Do you understand?
Hence Adonai's observation, "My people die for lack of
understanding."

Some theologians opine that the Messiah was referring
to the "rapture," which by itself is controversial. No, He was
not: "The world will not see me anymore" suggests that
Jesus will still "be here," of course, and everywhere, given His
Omnipresence, but physically invisible.

Question: if the Messiah was yet to ask for the Holy Spirit,
why did He say (In present tense), "He lives with you . . ." and
add later, "Before long, the world will not see Me, but you
will." How long is "[b]efore long"?

Was Christ Fully Man and Fully God? De-Divining Ultimate Divinity

What do people mean when they say that Christ was
fully man and fully God? Some of the answers can be
gleaned from the sermons presented through the years,
books written, and explanations offered daily at religious
services and Bible/Torah study classes. Alas, Christ has been

so thoroughly and completely humanized that hardly any divine characteristics remain in their original states. This de-divination has gone on for a long time and has been exploited by mankind, especially the antagonists of Christ, to denigrate God. It does appear that some preachers and Bible teachers could not wait to paint the portrait of Christ from their diseased imaginations and to present the Savior of the world as any twenty-first-century young adult thirsting for the fleshly, the profane, and the forbidden. Some pastors, to their own damnation, illustrate Him as like any one of us who struggles with temptations. Determined to humanize Yeshua, such loudspeakers of Satan teach that the omnipotent One, who, as we know, created mankind and everything that was made, had to be taught discipline, knowledge, and wisdom. Such is pure idiocy!

If the Holy Bible recorded that, "in the beginning was the Word, and the Word was with God, and the Word was God," why do people still say that the Word, Christ, who is God, had to be taught anything at all? They have neglected the Teacher and Counselor, the Holy Spirit, and have turned their ears to their own deceived, diseased minds, to fables and doctrines of demons. Mankind has fallen into paganism, theophany, transcendental mysticism, classical humanism, and modern secular humanism in attempting to understand the Godhead. What have they dredged up? A hydra-headed monstrosity, a quasi-Christian, paganistic acronym that looks and sounds like the Teachings of Christ but is something else altogether. The "wisdom" of "if it looks and quacks like a

215

duck, it is a duck" has failed mankind. If it looks like a duck, it may actually be a wooden duck decoy.

Yes, the incarnated Messiah looked like a man, but He was not a man. "The cloak does not make a monk." Neither does a uniform make a police officer. If a cop is to infiltrate a gang, he or she must wear street clothes and go under cover. The body that Yeshua, the Messiah, "borrowed" was but His earthly "costume."

The satanic virus of secular humanism has overwhelmed mankind's weakened immune system, infecting all traditional Christian churches and households, under the very noses of leaders and parents, who themselves have been infected. The victims are unaware that blasphemy within them and around them has gone viral. They do not even suspect their insidious disconnection from the One True God.

Christ Understands Our Temptations Only Because He Was Tempted?

Nonsense! This pinto pagan idea, crystallized in the devil's distillery, means that Christ can understand our problems and temptations *because* He, too, was tempted by Satan, tortured by the Romans, and forsaken by Adonai, His Father. We have to be patient, charitable, and fair, even tolerant, but we must pray and plead that no one believes in or preaches this age-old slander of the Divine One. The notion being presented is that Christ needed to have experienced all our experiences, including being forsaken by His Father, in order to feel our pain. Believing that concept is tantamount to calling Adonai, our Precious Lord, an equivocator. Those who do so will be utterly damned—unless, of course, they repent of their wickedness and ask God's forgiveness.

Incoherency

The inconsistency between the Infallible, Immutable Word of Adonai, on one hand, and many believers' understandings and applications of the Word, on the other hand, creates an unsettling state of anarchy. It should be disturbing to all true believers when people claim that Yeshua, the Omnipotent, whom we know to be God, had to be taught things, had to experience temptation, lack, pain, and treachery to be able to understand what we, as humans, are going through. Where is Omniscience in this? Did the contemporaries of Christ not marvel at His Unbounded Wisdom and Knowledge? When Jesus Messiah spoke, did they not quiz themselves as to where such Wisdom and Knowledge came from? Did they not, in their wonderment, ask, "Is this not the son of Joseph the carpenter and Mary, and are his brothers and sister not so and so?"

If anyone would know whether Christ was "a student," it would be His contemporaries, right? But wait a minute. At what age did His formal and informal education begin? Did He graduate? When? Was it before or after His professorial appearance in the temple, addressing the greatest scholars of theology? Though it was common in Jewish culture and religion to allow a thirteen-year-old to read from the book of the law during his bar mitzvah, it was not at all common for a teenage boy to lecture professors on spiritual matters. Jesus was not revered and thus granted special status because He was a child prodigy, always curious to learn more. No, He Was—and Is—Divine, the One Who Has Always Known Everything.

Was the Venerable Messiah Simply a Genius?

It cannot be said in Truth that Christ was simply a genius, a prodigy, one whose dexterity and versatility could be as "mysterious" and "wondrous" as the genius of Mozart, Picasso, or Einstein. O Lord, illuminate our hearts and minds, and may your Spirit guide our footsteps and grant us wisdom. Amen.

If Christ's historic temple appearance does not cause raised eyebrows, let us try this response to His parents' question after He went missing for a number of days. "Why were you looking for me, don't you know that I have to work in my Father's house?" (Luke 2:49). To everyone but the Virgin Mary and Joseph, Christ was the legitimate son of Joseph. Which father was He then talking about, and who told Him that He had work to do in said Father's *house*?

We imagine that the people during Christ's days on earth were not so disturbed as in our time by a child's reaction to having been adopted. The young Messiah knew that His earthly father was Joseph. As well, He knew that He was the Son of God the Father, with whom He Was, and Is, One, and that He came to earth on a very special Mission. It did not matter that the Jewish leaders did not believe the Holy Spirit connection in the Immaculate Conception. Everyone in that community knew that Joseph, after his initial rejection of Mary, must have gained new information and then accepted responsibility for her pregnancy. If Joseph had not claimed responsibility, the self-righteous judges probably would have had her stoned to death. It would have aggravated the situation and enraged the Jews even more if Mary and Joseph had tried to explain Adonai's role in the conception.

So for Christ, Joseph was a kind of foster dad, a sort of cover-up, surrogate dad, but the Prophetic Words that Jesus spoke were not just spiritual lingo. They were His own, a fact testified to by His experienced and discerning audience, who said that He spoke like one with authority rather than quoting or referencing a rabbinical scholar to substantiate His teaching. The Venerable Messiah understood the Whole Mystery, allowing things to take their foreordained course. Mary and Joseph must have lived in fear because of the proximity of Heaven to their mortal, sinful hearts.

You see, in mankind's carnal zeal to understand the mysteries of Divinity, especially the Divinity of Christ, people have inadvertently, some innocently, others mischievously and intentionally, allowed intellectualism and rationalism inspired by classical humanism to becloud their hearts and minds. Brethren, be free from this bondage in Yeshua's Name. Amen.

Fortifying the Adversaries' Arsenal against Christ and His Body

Outside the inspiration and tutelage of the Holy Spirit, the danger inherent in trying to understand and explain the Divinity of Christ has manifested itself in the porous, superficial testimonies made by so many believers in and followers of Christ. These modernists corrode traditional Christian faith, denigrating rather than elevating God the Divine, with prevarications and contradictions that render the Holy Bible inaccurate, inconsistent, and incoherent. Worse still, we allow such antagonists to hold on to and disseminate their misconceptions and clichés. They neither exalt God nor edify the True Church of Christ. We turn the other cheek. Perhaps we should, as Jesus said. But at the same time, must we not be champions for the True Christ?

How Do Christians Do This?

Christians arm—or, in effect, become—the enemy, principally by questioning everything and not believing or accepting plain biblical truths. Here is a good example: if the apostle Paul was confident in his claim and loudly declared, 'Brothers, I want you to understand that the Gospel I preach is not something that man made up. I did not receive it from any man; nor was I taught it; rather, I received it by revelation from Jesus Christ" (Galatians 1:11), why should anyone claim that Saul was taught these things by men? And why should they insist that Christ, the Omnipotent One, was taught "these things"? Apostle Paul, whose type there is none in our days, declared that what he knew was given to him by his Lord and Master, Jesus, the Messiah. Contemporary Christians, who are spiritual Lilliputians compared to any of the apostles of Christ, try to lecture the Lecturer. What arrogance! What impudence! Brethren, God descries haughtiness!

Whatever your view is on the issue of Christ, His Divinity, and His "man-ness," do not let the man-made Christ become a hindrance to your knowledge and understanding of, and surrender to, the Father, the Son, and the Holy Spirit.

Cerebral versus Spiritual Understanding of the Godhead

In order to convey our thesis vividly, I must think like secular humanists and say some things that might be considered blasphemous. Yes, it does take extraordinary nerve to think and say some of the things that have been said about Adonai and Yeshua. Trying to understand this "God-man" concept and the attributes of Christ cerebrally and logically is an exercise in futility. Attempting to resolve the issue through a combination of the empirical and the spiritual is also futile, like trying to blend oil and water.

Many Christians and people who denigrate them have proffered such "solutions" so often that they have become commonplace, accepted as dogma and liturgy, despite their sociological and theological inaccuracies. What pollution!

Satan and His Fallen Angels Know the Messiah Better Than Most Average Christians

When Paul and Barnabas were mistaken for gods (Acts. 13), they protested, went as far as stripping their clothes and pleading with the people not to worship them, for obvious reasons: they were human beings who chose to obey God and not be like Herod, who soaked in men's praises and failed to stop them from offering him worship that belonged to Adonai. Herod was consumed by giant worms (Acts: 12). Paul rebuffed worshippers many times, as was his custom, and Peter, when he went to the house of Cornelius, forbade the man's worshipping of him, saying exactly as Paul and Barnabas had done (Acts 15:16): "I am but a man like you . . . ." (Acts 10:26)

Did Satan know that it was Adonai Yeshua before he tempted Him? Yes. That was why he questioned the Venerable and Omniscient Christ: "If Thou be the Son of God . . . ." Consider Christ's answer: "Thou shall not tempt the Lord thy God . . ." nor worship any other but Adonai. It becomes clearer why the apostles had a custom of firmly rejecting worship from men, knowing that worship and adoration belong to God alone. A question arises here: "If

Christ is not God and was being worshipped as a man, which He was in many instances, as in the case of Legion, why did He not stop them, saying, as He had taught or commanded His followers, as Paul and Barnabas said, "Do not worship me because I am just a man of like passion as you are." He did not do so, for it would amount to lying. He never ceases to be the Lord our God, Adonai Yeshua. Do you remember that Mary washed His feet with her tears, wiped them with her hair, and anointed Him with oil from her alabaster box? What drove her to such a degree of humble worship?

If Yeshua Adonai is not God Always, why did God instruct the Magi as He did, and why did they worship a "mere human child"? Was their worship for who He was not, but would be, or was it for the Divinity, wearing a "cloak" of flesh that men and women who walk by sight might behold Him Who had existed from time immemorial, before there was time? If you do not believe anyone else, believe Him when He says, "Before Abraham, I am, and I and My Father are One . . . if you have seen Me, then you have seen Him."

The demons operating in the sons of Sceva knew Christ, whom Paul preached about, but the charlatans, they did not know. Does that not conclusively illustrate that demons are more sensitive to the Presence of the Godhead than are modern Christians? We in our adult Christian conviction are still asking the Messiah to show us the Father, and we have, to the detriment of our Faith, contradicted ourselves as to who Jesus Christ really is, even after He authoritatively said to His Apostles, "If you have seen me, you have seen my Father . . .

I and My Father are One . . . ." What else, who else, are we waiting for, to endorse the Infallible Word of the Creator?

Did not the legion of demons know who Christ was? Did they see a mere man, or were they in the Glare of Immaculate Holiness? Listen to Mark: "As the possessed man saw Him [Jesus Christ], from afar, he ran towards Him, **prostrated before Him, and worshipped Him.** 'Why hast thou come to put an end to us before the appointed time?'" (Mark 5: 15). Did they see another powerless, ordinary man, one of those who had tried abortively to bind them, or did they see God, the only One who can "put an end to us" before or after the appointed time? When the villagers saw what the Lord had done, they, for various reasons, raised their voices, and unanimously asked God to leave them alone. Complete insensitivity to the proximity of Heaven to earth. Spiritual blindness. What did John the Immerser see when he reverently asked the Messiah, "Why hast Thou come that I may baptize you . . . ?" (Matthew 4:15-17).

Christ Abdicated His Throne

Christ's abdication of His Heavenly Throne to sojourn among us for the purpose of our redemption may confuse us, not because it could not be done or was not done, but because it is so unlike us humans willingly to step down from a unique position of honor and power. We do not like to relinquish the opulence and thrill of royalty or other high station to those of lower station. Power intoxicates and corrupts most who have acquired it, and, alas, absolute power corrupts absolutely.

Totally transcending what we know about human power and corruption, when God the Omnipotent Messiah came to earth as Jesus of Nazareth, He came—and remained—in the form of man of pure Humility, Grace, Kindness, Compassion, and Love—the likes of whom mankind had never seen, nor will ever see again, until Christ Himself returns. We should not think less of ourselves for finding it difficult to comprehend this Wondrous Mystery.

If Billionaire Bill Gates Should Abdicate His Status!

Let us further illustrate Christ's Utter Uniqueness by considering the very generous charitable work of Bill and Melinda Gates. One of the richest couples in the world, the Gateses recently energized their global humanitarian projects by injecting twenty-five billion dollars of their own money in addition to encouraging other donors. Mr. Gates even resigned his leadership position in his multi-billion-dollar empire in order to focus on charity work. To work most effectively with the poor of the world, what must they do? All too often, well-intentioned charities pour money into poor communities without the vision and planning necessary to achieve lasting impact. As well, all too often, people of such immense means are so insulated from the people they wish to aid that they cannot realistically interact with the poor and determine how best to help them improve their lives.

As multi-billionaires Bill and Melinda Gates, regardless how well meaning, must work very hard to become credible in the eyes of the poor and of the governments of poor nations. Even if the Gateses sleep on the streets with the homeless, panhandle with them, and scavenge trash cans with them, they remain, do they not, Bill and Melinda Gates—no offense intended.

To their credit, their five-point plan for aiding the poor and for encouraging others to do so, as well, does have the potential for long-term impact. One great example is their asking, What is one of the most basic human needs worldwide? The answer? Clean water! Such a specific basic goal does embody visionary thinking and planning. The Gateses do provide massive direct support for very practical clean-water projects, such as the drilling of village wells and the eventual invention and manufacture of a non-electric toilet that will actually transform human waste into clear, clean water. They support other thoughtful programs, too, that are designed to aid people in becoming self-sufficient farmers or entrepreneurs. And they spend a great deal of time in the field, interacting with the poor as well as working hands-on with governments and charitable agencies to help people develop true self-sufficiency.

Precisely What Christ Did

We do not intend, of course, to compare the human Gateses with the Divine Jesus Christ. While Mr. and Mrs.

Gates are to be commended for their vision, planning, and generosity with time and money, they continue to be identified as the human multi-billionaires that they are. Yeshua the Messiah "left" His Heavenly Throne and totally assumed the form of a street man to be able to minister to those who were disenfranchised—physically, economically, socially, politically, spiritually. "Foxes have dens and birds have nests, but the Son of Man has no place to lay his head" (Luke 9:58). Yes, that is what the Messiah did. If Christ had come as the Messiah whom the traditional Jews were expecting, a man of great power and visible glory, such as Bill and Melinda Gates the multi-billionaires, His successes would have been vastly limited and less sacrificial. Only those who are not clad in rare purple linen, only those who do not live in palaces and do not ride in gold-trimmed chariots or exotic limited-edition automobiles, are truly qualified to come to the "banquet" that has been set for the poor.

The Messiah Fulfilled the Holy Scriptures

The risks taken by Jesus and the Gateses would have to be inspired by one thing and only one thing: love. Yes, consider the grave danger to Mr. and Mrs. Gates should a gang of hoodlums discover their true identity. For the same reason, Adonai had to "hide" His true identity, layered under the stratum of humanity. He was perceived wrongly by most people, who saw him, not as who He Is, but, rather, as who He was not. For this reason, in the mind of mankind, He had to die. But death, where is your sting? Grave, where is your victory over the Son of God?

It must be heartening to Bill and Melinda Gates, knowing the truth about themselves and their immense wealth and influence, knowing that the drama of their whole undertaking will soon end.

An Actor's Perspective on Abdication

A movie actor made the point succinctly after the closed-door screening of his production drew not only ovation but also pools of tears from the critics and special invitees. The movie in which he was protagonist was about some suffering tribe in the jungles of South America. Even though it was his acting ability that unraveled the truth about this tribe, he was not insulated from the impact of the highly emotional story, which provoked fresh streams of sorrow in this actor.

Seeing this extensive outpouring of sentiment, the press asked, "How were you able to perform in this story if it still has such a gripping, nerve-wracking influence on you?" His answer would be sufficient for any true believer in and follower of the Messiah, should the world ask why we believe. The actor responded, "I survived the torture of the reality of these people's existence because I constantly reminded myself that I was only an actor, and that this whole thing would soon be over, and that I would be returning to my multimillion-dollar home and my most priceless possessions, but especially to civilization . . . to my wife and my children. That hope kept me going."

Does the hope of eternal bliss with our Heavenly Father keep you believing in and following after the Messiah? We are pilgrims, my friends. Let us not overcrowd our space or overburden ourselves. We really do not need all these toys that the culture makes available to us—because the entrance into eternal *shalom* is narrow.

The Gifts of Wisdom, Art, and Science

The Omniscient God knew yesterday before it became today, and today when it was only tomorrow, and tomorrow before it would be today, then yesterday. Nothing is a mystery to Him, not even His Infinitude. To enable us to unravel some of the mysteries surrounding our lives, to know God, and to understand the things that He has done, Adonai has endowed us with the potential to cultivate knowledge through art and science and to achieve wisdom. Art and science are not our inventions but God's provisions. When used constructively, as directed by Adonai, they help illuminate the depths of our mind and soul. Alas, these gifts are being abused. We have allowed them to become our measure of God's quality and ability and of eternity. The gifts also provide us with reasons to think that mankind is God, "knowing all things." Ridiculous! Adonai, the Omniscient Giver, provides these gifts of art and science, not to vilify Him, but to glorify Him.

Science is one of the many keys that Almighty God has made available to us for unlocking and demystifying unknowns in the universe. But science does not know all things and was not intended to be the measure of all things as some thinkers have claimed. For only Adonai, whose Name is blessed and exalted above all blessings and praise, is Omniscient. We are not!

Chapter 5

THE EPILOGUE

How Does It Feel to Be on Our Own? Forsaken?

How do we feel when we are abandoned by the ones we love? Feelings of emptiness are the way of the flesh and cannot be expurgated from our character. Breaking promises to or forsaking one another has been rationalized as a vital skill for survival, for self-preservation. Unchecked, this insensitivity has become a virus that is destroying our families, marriages, and other relationships. Our promises have become nothing but words spat without thought. What's more, we have credited this human frailty to God by deifying ourselves and humanizing the Divinity! What insidious, dangerous frivolity!

We have explored contemporary culture's persistent accusations of God as an equivocator who promises not to forsake us believers and then fails to keep His promises. What impetuosity we humans display!

Have We Received Adonai's Gift?

It is hard, sometimes impossible, to understand modern-day Christianity, especially its interpretation of Holy Writ. What makes a man or woman a Christian, a believer in and follower of Christ? We have consciously elected to call Him Lord and Master, recognize His redemptive work on the cross, put all our trust, hope, and life in His Hands, and turn our backs on the sinful world. The "old man dies and a brand-new man, made in the new image, that of the Master, is born." This mysterious rebirth cannot occur unless the Holy Spirit calls us and directs us to Christ, granting us the knowledge and wisdom to recognize Him as the One and Only Mediator, the One and Only Way, and to place our trust in Him. Brethren, have we answered the Call?

Now, can God give us anything without first giving us Himself? "Whatever you ask me through my Son [His gift], I will do for you" (Paraphrase John 14:14). According to A. W. Tozer, God always imparts Himself with His gift. If we prayed for the granting of all gifts listed in the New Testament and God assented without placing Himself within the gifts, those gifts would destroy the beneficiary. Why? Because the benefactor would be, not God, but Satan!

What is God's greatest gift? Himself in Christ—but "wrapped" in human flesh that He may "look like us" and live among us in order to Model Righteousness for us to emulate.

Does Our Religion Interfere with Our Private, Everyday Life?

During the period of our service as house parents at a Christian establishment, my wife, Connie, once asked our foster sons how many minutes per day they thought about God. After a long but uneasy silence, Al (not the real name), the most outspoken and seemingly the most religious said, "In all honesty, none." The next said the same, and the next, "Me neither." What the boys actually meant was that they never specifically meditated on God, but they knew God was working in their behalf.

Do those of us who claim to be believers in and followers of the Venerable Christ think about and commune with our Heavenly Father each and every day? If we do not, then we must presume ourselves to be self-reliant, self-sufficient, and self-sustaining. If so, then in what sense have we turned our lives over to His Divine Keeping and been Saved? How long can a fish survive out of water? Does an electric light bulb shine after its connecting wires have been severed? Adonai is the Unseen Dynamic Force that gives life to a Christian—but only if we grow our tap roots deeper, into the nurturing soil that is God.

I have been waiting for this moment to share with you an especially soul-searching observation of A. W. Tozer. This article of his is a gold mine.

Emeka Anonyuo, Ph.D.

"Bold Men Needed in the Warfare of the Soul" (A.W. Tozer)

(Author's note: If Pastor Tozer were teaching, preaching, and writing today, in all likelihood he would say and write "men and women.")

The Church at this moment needs men; the right kind of men; bold men. The talk is that we need revival, that we need a new baptism of the Spirit—and, God knows, we must have both, but God is not going to revive mice, He will not fill rabbits with the Holy Ghost.

We languish for men who feel themselves expendable in the warfare of the soul; who cannot be frightened by threats of death because they have already died to the allurements of the world. Such men will be free from the compulsions that control and squeeze weaker men.

This kind of freedom is necessary if we are to have Prophets in our pulpits again, instead of mascots. These types of free man will serve God and mankind with motives too high to be understood by the rank and file of religious entertainers who today shuttle in and out of the sanctuary.

These men will make no decisions out of fear, take no course out of a desire to please, accept no service for financial considerations, perform no religious act out of mere custom nor will they allow themselves to be influenced by the love of popularity or the desire for reputation.

The true Church has never sounded out public expectations before launching their crusades, their leaders heard from God; they knew their Lord's will and did it. Their people followed them— sometimes to triumph, often to insults and public persecutions—and their sufficient reward was the satisfaction of being right, in a wrong world . . . .

A True Christian Is a Man or Woman Carrying a Cross

Many Christians who have tried to remember how they answered the altar call have said that they were not sure what to expect and not sure how their future was going to be impacted, or they never thought about it, or they were too excited or confused to think about any one thing. One message most of them heard and were made to believe was that "old things would pass away, and new things would take their place." By this they meant that their former problems would dissipate as soon as they became "born again." No one explained to them that, when the Messiah calls us, He demands full obedience and commitment, demands that we pick up our own cross and walk in the footsteps of our Master. A dreadful thought, isn't it, should we seriously consider aspiring to follow and be like the Messiah!

A. W. Tozer said that one picture of a true Christian is a man carrying a cross—who no longer controls his destiny. That cross becomes to him an all-absorbing passion, an overwhelming force. There is but one thing he can do, Tozer continued, "that is, move on towards the place of crucifixion!" (G. Smith, *Renewed Day by Day*)

"If any man will come after me, let him deny self, take up his cross and follow me," says the Lord. Note that Christ did not say that such a man should take up Christ's cross, but his own cross. This does not call for an ordinary commitment, but for a covenant, for total allegiance to and reliance on God the Divine.

The cross sometimes may, and will, get too heavy, causing tripping and falling under its weight as we get closer to our Golgotha. Our Simon of Cyrene will be none other than the Lord and Master of the universe Himself. We may receive encouragement from our brethren, even unbelievers, but it will be only the Christ that will lift our crosses from our shoulder and place them on His own. At this point on our journey, we will be faced by choices: to let Him carry our cross or to resist and reject His offer of assistance.

My son *Chidiomimi* (God Is Unfathomable) called me one evening just to say these words: "Dad, it is being taught that Jesus Christ will carry our crosses. I think that is wrong because He carries both the cross and its bearer . . . Awesome."

The Desire Not to Be Saved

The choice we make at this point will be determined by our sensitivity to Adonai's Presence. The lack of this sensitivity is usually caused by egotism and haughtiness, which lead to ignorance of His Word, thereby hardening the heart and engendering non-recognition or realization of God's love for us.

Commenting on a question about mankind's resistance to God's request to control our lives, Gail Johnson, founder and one-time pastor of the True Gospel Sabbath School of Faith, said, "It is very hard to understand why some people that suffer from various kinds of diseases would rather they were not healed/cured/helped. They seem to disdain those who have the potential for offering assistance." Why is it? she asked; after all, God has counseled us to "be still" and know that He is God and then to see our salvation.

"Be still and know that I am God." Is it possible that many Christians enjoy suffering? Have they, like many people, gotten so used to affliction that they do not really care about Redemption? Are we sometimes so acquainted with sorrow that we wallow in unhappiness and self-pity? Sometimes, the depth of our angst frustrates any efforts by the most determined, charitable humanitarians to reach us with good intentions. Is it that, after being so long in the throes of negative forces and experiences, we become immune to discomfort and just consciously adopt or feign insensitivity to its existence? Ask the psychologists, or, better still, ask God!

It has been suggested that such people who discourage any attempt to encourage them towards Christ are either engrossed in a love affair with a condition, not really caring about liberty from it, or are afraid of going through the dreaded hangover associated with letting go of an old habit. That makes sense. Alcoholics and drug addicts dread the agony of withdrawal cold turkey: sweats, chills, shakes, hallucinations, you name it. Those gnawing experiences are inevitable for any determined sick person who chooses the way of restoration and transformation—unless, of course, God intervenes with a miracle. Might this same sort of fear and dread cause so many people, though aware of their carnality and need of salvation, to flee from the thought of joining the Messiah?

Momentary Discomfort versus Eternal Distress

Do some cancer patients fear the side effects of chemotherapy and radiation more than they fear death? Do some allow their tumor to grow and metastasize simply because they dread the scalpel? Such paralyzing thoughts nearly stopped me from having much-needed eye surgery. My redemption came as a song out of the Book of Psalms: "The

Lord is my light and my salvation, the Lord is the strength of my life. And I will not be afraid, yes, I will not be afraid because the Lord is my light, the Lord is my life, and the Lord is life" (27:1). I was told that I muttered the song, sometimes audibly, during the surgery. *Baruch Adoni*. Blessed be the Lord my God!

In much the same way, backsliding Christians and unbelievers, comfortable in the pleasurable lust in which they live, become immune to the Presence and Voice of the Holy Spirit. Their hearts, according to Holy Scriptures, become seared and calloused. But there is a solution, a way out. Everyone can find it in the Word of God. This Way is illuminated by His Light, the Light of the World, Jesus the Messiah.

The Calloused Heart Feels Nothing, Desires the Wind, and Produces the Whirlwind

We find this to be one of the more significant reasons why transformation, though touted and mouthed, is very hard to accomplish: the calloused mind or heart feels nothing, desires nothing, produces nothing constructive, and dies ignorant and insensitive to everything (L. Ravenhill). That is why the Power of God, although pervading every space, infusing every subatomic particle, remains unrecognized and untapped by so many. That is why mere fallible, frail mankind can put his finger in the face of God Almighty, misrepresent His Word, and accuse Him.

Emeka Anonyuo, Ph.D.

Our Theme Music: Adonai Does Not, Did Not, and Will Never Forsake the Righteous

With overwhelming evidence and testimonies from both the living and the dead, we conclude that, if a lie was told, it was not Adonai who told it, for God does not lie. If someone equivocated, it was not Adonai, for God does not equivocate. If someone was forsaken, it was not by Adonai, for God does not forsake anyone who chooses the path of Righteousness and Salvation. It was mankind who forsook Adonai, just as it was mankind who forsook Yeshua the Messiah. As we conclude, we especially confirm our total rejection of the oxymoronic idea that God the Father forsook or would ever forsake Christ the Son. To forsake His Son, we insist, would be tantamount to forsaking the righteous and, as well, forsaking Himself, for God the Father, God the Son, and God the Holy Spirit are One. Righteous humans are "dead" to human selfhood and the fallible world. We are filled with the Holy Spirit. Christ lives within us. We live for Him. God Loves and Keeps us, His flock.

Adonai never forsakes the righteous. He said to Joshua, "Moses my servant is dead. Now, you and all these people, get ready to cross the Jordan River into the land that I am about to give to them . . . As I was with Moses, so I will be with you. I will never leave you nor forsake you" (Joshua 1:2–5). He did not forsake them. He will not forsake them. The state of Israel lives as unparalleled evidence of God's Faithfulness.

Most importantly, Adonai did not forsake Christ. It is both foolish and dangerous to put words in the mouth of God simply because we have become spiritually complacent and unable to discern the Truth in His Word.

We know the Truth: "Until heaven and earth disappear, not the smallest letter, not the least stroke of a pen shall by any means disappear from the Law" (Matt. 5:18).

There were and are, however, clear prerequisites for qualifying for this Eternal Protection and Provision.

> Be careful to obey all the Law my servant Moses gave to you, do not turn from it, to the right or to the left, that you may be successful wherever you go. Do not let this book of the law depart from your mouth; meditate upon it day and night, that you may be careful to do **everything** written in it. Then, you will be prosperous and successful. (Joshua 1:6–8; my emphasis).

God did not, does not, and will never forsake the righteous. He did not forsake the Messiah. We hope this book has cast some light on the path to full, true understanding of why Jesus Christ, the Venerable One, cried out, "My Lord, My Lord, why have you forsaken me?"

Did the venerable Messiah not say that He would not leave us till the end of time? When would this be? Why did He say this since He had told His apostles that He would be betrayed and crucified and ascend into Heaven? Ascending into Heaven denotes separation from them. So why did He make that promise? He made it because another member of the Godhead, the Holy Spirit, would be eternally in attendance. The Holy Scriptures say that the most dreaded weapon of offense by the devil, death, cannot separate us from the Love and Presence of God. Death, where is your victory? God, the Holy Spirit, Never Separates from us.

Brethren, God does not lie. He Is where we are, so that when we depart this mortal existence, we will be Where He Is.

"Eli, Eli, Lama sabbacthani," My Lord, My Lord, Why Have You Forsaken Me?

The Last Word

What Yeshua Messiah, said at Golgotha shortly before He gave up the Ghost, "Father, Father, why hast Thou forsaken me?" was not accusatory. Neither was it the desperate cry of a distressed and anxious man who was abandoned by a previously doting Father. Saying otherwise is a heinous misrepresentation of the Divine Event, a misrepresentation that challenges the very character and Omniness of Adonai.

I, who embarked on this honorable, if perilous, journey of upholding the Whole Truth, without equivocation, unapologetically declare that Adonai never forsakes the righteous. I hope that, as you have traveled with us on this journey, your faith in the Steadfastness of God has been confirmed. It is comforting and energizing, is it not, to know in our heart, mind, and spirit that our God, Adonai, does not forsake anyone, not even the unrighteous.

God Will Never Forsake His Children: Israel as Example

Whenever we see the State of Israel on the world map, we are reminded, are we not, that God still loves all His children: Jews, Christians of all denominations, Muslims, Hindus, Sikhs, Buddhists, and even pagans, agnostics, and atheists. Yes, He does. Why do we highlight Israel as a testament to God's Steadfast, Unconditional Love? Because, no matter what they have believed or done, He still loves the Jewish people. True, since the time of the early Israelites, Jews have sustained themselves as children of God, even in the face of horrific persecution. At the same time, no people have rebelled more against His Commandments. Yet Adonai Loves them with the passionate love of the mother wolf. And God is not partial. He Loves us all with the same Intensity.

The nation of Israel, "The Apple of God's Eye," is Adonai's model, an illustration of His unconditional love for all peoples, even the prodigal son. Adonai gave His Word not to forsake us, and He watches it closely to perform it. That is why He set His Word above His Name. We may forsake God, but God will never forsake us. Of course, we must understand that forsaking Adonai is spiritual madness. He did say that He will not contend with the spirit of mankind forever.

No matter our race, color, nationality, or current creed, we can all achieve Salvation and Eternal Life: by believing totally in the GodHead; by choosing to obey Adonai's Commandments as revealed in the Holy Scriptures; by loving Him and putting our trust in Him; by humbling ourselves, confessing our sins, and requesting forgiveness; and by accepting Yeshua the Messiah into our hearts and following Him—for He is *the Way of Salvation*. Praise be to God Almighty, for He Will See us Through!

APPENDICES
APPENDIX ONE

Betrayed and Forsaken in Marital Relationship

Fear and suspicion of being betrayed by one's life-partner casts an immense dark shadow on a marriage. Actual betrayal is even more destructive, especially when it leads to divorce, a treachery that, in contemporary times, has become a pandemic. Frighteningly, this odious cultural phenomenon mimics the relationship that many Christians have with Adonai Yeshua, the Divine Bridegroom.

A marital relationship, which should emulate that of Yeshua Messiah and the Church, His Body, begins with two human beings of different sexes, as commanded by Adonai, choosing each other from a population of over five billion men and women, and swearing an oath to live together, to love and cherish the other in times of sickness and health, for richer or poorer, for better or worse, till death do they part. Their unity is cemented and consummated, and the two become one, no longer two separate beings. Over them, the pastor, representing godly authority, speaks these words: "What God has joined together, let no one put asunder."

Emeka Anonyuo, Ph.D.

What God Has Joined Together, Let No One Put Asunder?

Who is listening? All too often, these ceremonial words, as with other passages of holy ritual, are recited quickly, absentmindedly, without the necessary thought required for one to hear, process, and consider adopting them and living by them. Not long after the honeymoon, the first adversarial winds of testing blow in the direction of the newly wedded couple. Recent statistical studies show that life's storms blow about 60 percent of marriages to their destruction on rocks and reefs. Much desired conjugal bliss and financial stability are swept away, leaving in their wake a backwash of unpaid bills, insomnia, broken dreams, and depression—in some cases, even suicide or homicide or both.

Many factors contribute to the whirling winds that eventually demolish so many marriages, even Christian ones. Topping the list is the couple's attitude toward God and His Commandments.

Of course, reasons for dysfunction in relationships vary from person to person, but the results are much the same: separation of one from the other, physically, emotionally, spiritually. So often, couples, feeling disconnected and distraught, fight like demons about who said what or who did that or who is going to get the microwave. They hire lawyers to battle for them—no holds barred—with courtroom theatrics. All is fair game— even the kids who once blessed their blissful union. Where does love go? What about "Till death do us part"?

Such feelings and behavior roil up when trust is broken and people experience betrayal. Those who cuddled and shared the most intimate moments now become dreaded mortal enemies in a legacy of greed, frailty, and treachery. The man and woman who should love each other, as the Venerable Christ loves the church, having died for it, now become each other's nemesis, obsessed with trashing what was once divine.

Christ, the Model Bridegroom

Just as many couples allow life's storms to wreak havoc with their marriage, even their lives, many Christians allow similar dissolution of their relationship with Christ—although with a very significant difference: Jesus, the Divine Bridegroom, never, ever, even for a moment, falters in keeping His Vows. His Pure Divine Love Emanates from Him without conditions—to everyone, whether righteous or unrighteous. Of course, His Unconditional Love does not mean that we should continue our irreverence and disobedience to God's commands. We become His own, after all, by transcending the pitfalls of "self" and allowing Him, the resurrected Messiah, to live within us. It is His Presence that Purifies each of us and the bride, His Church. Never does He, or will He, forsake us or His Church. For His name is Immanuel, "God with us." When and for how long? Forever. For He is also Jehovah *Shammah*, "God who is always there." Indeed He is Omnipresent. To Him be all honor and glory, forever! Amen.

APPENDIX TWO

Is Adonai Present in Hell?

That question surely sounds sacrilegious, but the truth is that, after a closer look at the Omnipresence of Adonai, including its confirmation in King David's statement, "If I should make my home in Hell, You are there with me," I have come to realize that He is Present in hell. In fact, it is Adonai's very Presence there that makes hell a place of torture and suffering. Please don't yet throw stones at me. What I have come to realize is that His Presence in Satan's horrific domain exists at once with His absence. The condemned, tormented inhabitants suffer beyond suffering because, although the Serenity and Presence of God are so Imminent and Real, the inhabitants of Hell cannot possess even an inkling of it. This is called the "glass wall" concept. Every human being sees or feels this concept every day in the empirical world. We desire something, even covet it. In our mind, it is ours. But in reality, it is only our lustful, diseased mind conjuring up this reality as if it were accessible to us. A thirsty man is thirstier when there is an abundance of water within reach but he is prevented from acquiring even a drop to quench his thirst. This strategy has been craftily and successfully employed by torture experts to extract information from their captives. Sleep deprivation is an example. We know how it works: create a need, provide the need, but deny it to the needy.

Yahweh Adonai's Omnipresence means that He is everywhere at the same time, including whenever or wherever sin is being committed. Sin is sin because it is a blot on God's Immaculate Presence, and the presence of sin is, therefore, determined by God's Immaculate Presence. The presence of sin does not mean the absence of God. It means that our minds are so beclouded by what we desire (usually not according to the Word or Will of God), that we fail to see or feel God's Presence. Rather, we are drawn by the lure of Satan. It is God's Presence everywhere, always, that makes a Satan-lured man, swimming in fresh water, ever more thirsty than a righteous man in the Sahara desert during a sand storm.

APPENDIX THREE

Are There Still True Prophets of Adonai?

In this book, I refer extensively to the Holy Scriptures and intentionally limit my other references to just two major twentieth-century evangelists: A. W. Tozer and Leonard Ravenhill. I am familiar with many, many books by theologians, pastors, prophets, and puppets past and present. The bibliography is measly by design because, to me, as a messianic believer, so much Christian literature is biblically unsound and therefore untrustworthy. My exposure—and Connie's—to religious literature, especially Christian texts, has urged us to steer our vehicle away from precipitous spiritual canyons concealed by theological fog.

The corridors of power are now crowded with Christian combatants, who, like jostlers and hustlers, are stiffly locked in acrimonious, slanderous campaigns against one another. They are driven by vaulting ambition to stand in the spotlight on center stage. They employ arsenals of lethal weapons camouflaged by layers of Bible passages. Their utterances aim to decimate the image of rival religious organizations and obliterate the worth of those who dare to raise their voices in criticism or condemnation. They vigorously shoot for prominence and, like sex workers, flirt with and charm influential men and women to gain influence, power, and money.

Such harlotry is rampant in contemporary church affairs, compromising the Word of Yahweh Adonai. Today's church looks like a sociopolitical fraternity, practicing moral and spiritual debauchery, its demise imminent. What befuddles me is that those who noisily, jubilantly acclaim Adonai as Creator and declare faith in Lord Yeshua Messiah have, nonetheless, allowed themselves to be yoked to worldliness. The very same people who have been invited to the Lord's Banquet and who have been assigned enviable positions of leadership in religious circles have traded spirituality for eroticism and morality for postmodernist secular humanism.

This shameful moral and spiritual debauchery corrupts all denominations, their church leaders driven by unbridled lust for worldly power and possessions. As the bacchanal is reenacted, the counselor from hell instructs the revelers that "what is good for the goose is good for the gander." Recall the serpent's crafty enticement of Eve: "For God knows that when you eat of it your eyes will be opened, and you will be like God" (Genesis 3). A pastor once declared, "Christians should not let the devil take over every 'good thing'." Nothing sounds wrong with his point heard out of context. But, in context, he was arguing that the church should take hold of and utilize every worldly invention and lifestyle in the service and worship of God. The truth is that the devil, abhorring all good things, corrupts them wherever and whenever he can. Worldly things remain worldly. True children of the Almighty reject that which Satan has corrupted—unless, of course, it has since been Purified by Christ. "The Lord redeems, replaces, rejuvenates, revives, revamps, restores, reforms, reestablishes, resurrects . . . He makes all things new.

Spotlighting the Likes of A. W. Tozer and Leonard Ravenhill

Some servants of the Almighty God have answered the call, received the mantle and anointing, taken up the cross, and very closely followed the Master. They were men and, yes, women of great spiritual worth because they were empowered by God. They lived in the world of reality, thirsted for water and hungered for food, but they never mistook physical sustenance for spiritual endowment. They, like the Master, never mistook the elite for the elect. Though they had legitimate reasons—rejection by the general church family and affliction with physical, economic, and other hardships—to have thrown off the mantle and divorce the Bridegroom, Christ, they chose to wait patiently, just as servants anticipate the return of their master. Like the wise virgins, they kept their lamps trimmed and burning, looking forward, anxiously but patiently and prayerfully, to Christ's Divine Return.

We might assume that the roster of true religious leaders would be long, especially if we are counting all men and women worldwide who speak from pulpits, publish biblical commentaries, and organize crusades. What should be our criteria for measuring, evaluating, and scoring? The top criterion is how Christian leaders live and teach the Word of Adonai, the whole and wholesome Word of Truth. They must view the Omniness of God as Pure and Absolute, not adulterated or obsolete. Being anointed means so much more than the application of mere ointment. They must not deify mankind or humanize the Almighty. They must not select and cite only passages of the Word that justify their picture of God, Christ, and the Holy Spirit. And they must not view God's commandments as mere suggestions.

By searching far and wide, Connie and I have found servants of God who are delighted to serve rather than be admired celebrities with money and power. These model servants have sought solitude and found in it the Magnitude of the Infinitude of God. Their beliefs, attitudes, and practices have become aligned with the attributes of God. These servants have consciously traded their worldly nature to advance their spiritual nature, and they have discouraged their congregations from exalting them, for they know well the fate of Herod, eaten by worms for accepting the honor and glory due God. All who position themselves in society to receive the honor and glory reserved for Adonai face such a fate. God exalts the humble and detests haughtiness. Like Paul and Barnabas, who tore their robes and protested attempts by their fans to deify them, these selected servant-leaders would rather die than sin against God. They, like Moses, dare to stand between the imminent wrath of a righteous God and the foolishness and sin of the rebellious people in their keeping. They call it their duty to emulate the

Good Shepherd by going in search of the one missing sheep, and when they find it, in their joy and celebration, they are genuinely ecstatic. They feed their flock, not with grass, but with "*Pater nostra*," "*our Father.*"

These servants have no interest in producing miracles and signs that would spike their ratings and attract big audiences to their churches. Like the prophets of old, they fall on their faces before the Almighty God and confess their sins and those of their congregations, God's people. They make intercessions and even sometimes, like Moses, ask God to punish them on behalf of their flock. They use words like *awesome* only to try and communicate Adonai's Infinitude and not to describe the dexterity of a guitarist, the virtuosity of a violinist, or the fluidity of a soccer player. They encourage congregants to praise noisily, when appropriate, and otherwise to worship reverently, keeping silent and humbling themselves in the Presence of God. They do not allow the rising cost of dry cleaning or suitable clothing to prevent them from venerating God by kneeling or lying prostrate before Him. They do not amend or compromise the Word of God to placate sulking members who are uncomfortable with the Truth as given. They do not condone evil; they call sin sin and not merely a mistake. They insist that those who have consorted with the devil confess their wickedness and be cleansed or else be expelled from the fellowship of believers.

Faithful Remnant

These men and women, the faithful remnant, the true Christian leaders remaining after the hordes of unfaithful "leaders" have been culled, tremble at even the thought of humanizing Adonai and deifying themselves. God created mankind in His Own Likeness, and they know that God would not be flattered if they returned the favor by re-creating Him in their likeness. They do not teach that God opposes science but, rather, that science is a God-made instrument. When used constructively, it facilitates our understanding of the creation and confirms the Infinitude of God. They teach that "Thou shalt not . . ." means exactly that. Christians must abide by the Commandments or else they become disconnected from the Will, the perfect Will of God.

They are not necessarily products of seminaries, and they do not broadcast their identity with chic garb, pricey baubles, top-dollar limos, an adoring staff, an army of bodyguards, a mile-long résumé, and hard-to-pronounce, rainbow-colored titles such as the Esteemed Right Reverend Doctor Reginald Periwinkle Highfalutin, M.Th, D.D., professor, author, TV and radio personality, founder and president of the online men's haberdashery *Dress Up for Sunday*, prophet, pastor of the nation's largest and most entertaining church, true man of God.

They are prophets called and anointed by God to fulfill a mission. They do not entice congregants to "worship" them. They refuse to compete for the money and power of

Wall Street or the flamboyance and carnality of Hollywood. Because they serve as bridges between the people and God, their shoulders weigh heavily with concerns for the suffering of their congregants. Perversely, the charlatan celebrity preachers bear the weight of their own un-confessed sin and gaudy watches, bracelets, and necklaces. These prevent them from raising their hands and faces to God in surrender, supplication, worship, and adoration of Elohim.

The Comedian/Actor/Magician Minister

Secular-humanist ministers' galleries of global fashion elicit praise and money from enchanted spectator-congregants. The godly few who question the credentials of fraudulent men and women of God are ushered from church. Comedian-actor-preachers measure spiritual success by the bulk of one's wallet, the quality of one's gold and diamonds, the cost of one's automobile, and the market value of one's mansion. Those who do not have the requisite toys are looked upon as rejected by God.

Unlike movie-star preacher-pastors, the servant-pastors, who are called by God, anointed by the Holy Spirit, and guided by Christ, understand why the Messiah, the Venerable One, walked the earth in the flesh. Jesus said to Phillip and Thomas, "If you have seen me you have seen the

Father" (John 1:10). Righteous pastors know and celebrate, as all believer-followers do, that Christ is God. Boldly and confidently, they tell the world, "If you have seen me, you have seen Christ's servant. Follow me as I follow Him."

APPENDIX FOUR

We Repent, Pray, Fast, Expect Immediate Positive Response, and Soon Complain that "God Has Forsaken Us"

All too many Christians repent, pray, fast, and expect immediate positive response because they believe God is obligated to bless them and provide all the good stuff they need or desire. If the expected response does not follow immediately after the supplication, their microwave mentality kicks in with the conclusion that God has abandoned them, reneging on His promise never to forsake the righteous.

Yes, they ask and ask for multiplication of the storehouse, salvation of loved ones, success in business, and all such things. But rarely do they tell the Lord how wonderful He is. Or if they do, they do so as flattery and bribery. Rarely do they worship Him, praise Him, or Adore Him. Rarely do they acknowledge how impossible it would be to function without His Love. Repeatedly, they have made ambitious promises and failed to keep them. Yet they accuse Adonai of equivocation.

They believe that if they just mouth fashionable, pretty words about Christ being our "Lord and King," Abraham's blessings will immediately fall from the sky into their hands.

They expect a world without sorrows, roses without thorns, victory without battle. They make a fetish of God's promise, "Whatever you ask for through my Son, I will give to you" without conditions. A line in a song by the Crabb family says,

> "He never promised that the cross would not get heavy
> And the hill would not be hard to climb
> He never offered our victories without fighting
> But He said help would always come in time
> Just remember when you're standing in the valley of decision
> And the adversary says give in
> Just hold on, our Lord will show up
> And He will take you through the fire again"

Ignorance of God's Omniness

Such Christians and most of the rest of mankind live in a wilderness of our own making, cut off from the Presence of God. Why? Because we have failed to ask ourselves—and one another—this crucial question: Who is Adonai? And because, failing to muster the humility to trust God, we have not sought and listened to the Word of the Holy Spirit.

Indeed, what actually transpires when we ask "ourselves" a probing question? If we are true believers in the Father, the Son, and the Holy Spirit, and if we live righteously, we are filled with the Holy Spirit. Thus a question to "ourselves" is actually a question to the Holy Spirit within us. Asking a probing question or wrestling with a dilemma eventually results in a revelation. A Godly answer or solution eventually appears in our mind's eye. If, on the other hand, we are not true believer-followers and, therefore, are not filled with the Holy Spirit, when we ask "ourselves" a probing question or wrestle with a dilemma, an answer or solution can come only from our measly, fallible, mortal selves.

From Adam and Eve to Cain to King Saul to contemporary men and women, ignorance concerning God's Omniness has plagued us. All too many of us have assumed that God is unaware of what transpires on earth and relies on us to inform Him. Because we do not understand or trust His Omniness, we tend to lie to ourselves and question His dependability. We cover our faults, pretending that we are uncertain as to what God expects of us. We may ask God questions, but we do not hear His voice within us because we lack belief and trust that He Knows and Sees all things. We have disconnected ourselves from Him.

After Eve and Adam had disobeyed God by eating the forbidden fruit, He asked them what they had done. Eve answered, "The serpent gave me and I ate." Adam replied, "The woman you gave me, gave me and I ate." After Cain killed his brother, God asked, "Where is your brother, Abel?" Cain replied, "Am I my brother's keeper?" God asks such questions of mankind, not because He does not know what has transpired on earth, but because He Does Know—for He Knows All. He questions us in order that we might choose to reconnect with Him by admitting our transgressions, asking His Forgiveness, committing to righteousness, and being Restored to the Bosom of Christ. Glory to the Omniscient, Ever-Loving Adonai!

APPENDIX FIVE

Knowledge and Wisdom Came to the Apostles from Christ

The Apostles gained their knowledge and wisdom, not from university or seminary education, but from attentiveness to the Words and Actions of their Master, Jesus Christ. When they stumbled or fell, it was because they had strayed from the Messiah's Sage Precepts and Exemplary Deeds.

Sometime after Christ's crucifixion, Saul of Tarsus, a man of learning who persecuted early Christians, was walking on the road to Damascus. Suddenly he experienced the Presence and Power of the Lord, became transformed, and followed the way of the Messiah. Alas, however, his immense book learning often prevented his listeners from understanding his teachings. While his message was godly, his heavy, highfalutin words flew over people's heads or knocked them down. Peter testified to the righteousness of Paul's ministry and writings, saying that he spoke and wrote with the wisdom that God had given Him: "His letters contain some things that are hard to understand, which ignorant and unstable people distort as they do the other Scriptures, to their own destruction" (Peter 3:16).

At a later time, Paul stood before Porcius Festus, procurator of Judea, in defense of accusations brought against Paul by the Jews, who resented his Christian teachings. Because Paul's words completely befuddled and intimidated Festus, the procurator interrupted the defense. "You are out of your mind, Paul," Festus shouted. "Your great learning is driving you insane" (Acts 26:24). Paul's response was as godly as the very reasons why Festus felt intimidated by this godly man's knowledge, wisdom, and understanding of the inerrant Word of God: "Brothers, I want you to understand that the Gospel I preach is not something that man made up. I did not receive it from any man; nor was I taught it; rather, I received it by revelation from Jesus Christ" (Galatians 1:11).

Although Paul was divinely inspired to spread the Word of God, it seems that he sometimes failed to adapt his spoken and written words to his key mission: reaching out to potential believer-followers of the Messiah and persuading them to follow the Way of Righteousness and Salvation. Understandably, common people do not grasp and are intimidated by dense, high-flown speech or writing. Trying but failing to engage them can leave the door open to misunderstanding and temptation. Although Paul does surely stand as a steadfast, righteous spokesman for the Lord, sometimes his words have been misinterpreted.

For example, God commanded that believer-followers should not eat certain foods, especially a variety of meats and other foods traditionally sacrificed to idols. Some who have taken certain Bible passages out of context believe that Paul lifted the ban and instructed people to eat whatever their hearts desired, so long as they proffered thanksgiving to God. They misinterpret such isolated messages because they neglect to study the entire Bible and take into account the whole Truth. Clearly, there is danger inherent in narrow, selective reading and in forming unfounded conclusions.

Paul proclaimed truthfully that he had learned what he knew of godly righteousness and the Way, not from fallible earthlings, but from Christ, who informed and inspired every dimension of his life. Everything Paul said and wrote conveyed—or at least attempted to convey—the Pure, Immutable Nature of God and Christ. Peter, a senior apostle to Paul, testified that, yes, Paul's writings are often difficult to understand and, as well, people misunderstand him, to their own damnation, because they choose an errant path instead of the Way. The Truths of the Word are *spiritually* discerned.

APPENDIX SIX

Media Flood Perpetuates Unbiblical Teachings

> "Of making many books there is no end, and much
> study wearies the body."

—King Solomon, Ecclesiates12:12

In our time, more than ever, media of "communication" proliferate. Lectures, workshops, talk shows, books, magazines, films, CDs, DVDs. smart-phone apps, and who knows what, all teach all things "spiritual"—from how to be a favorite friend of God to how to build a spaceship guaranteed to transport a person to heaven. What is there to learn about the Venerable Adonai and His Omniness from this flood of mostly misinformation and propaganda? Much of the storm debris has little or nothing to do with God and pretty much everything to do with people's desire to have their say, get their name in lights, and join the exclusive but ever-expanding circle of Christian celebrities. These charlatanic opportunists are more attracted to the limelight of fame than the halo of righteousness. They present themselves as shepherds eager to pasture and protect their flock. But, instead, these materialistic exhibitionists tap dance, flaunting their theological brilliance—like today's politicians—all glitter and no gold. What ever happened to serving God's children and the public good?

As an enticement, they devise a labyrinth in whose frightening shadows they pretend to conceal God. With this ploy, the allure of a dark mystery, they hook their audience and promise an explanation in good time. The problem, of course, is that, because of their skewed values, beliefs, and attitudes, their arrogant imaginings produce a distorted view of God. The God that emerges from the shadows of their labyrinth is not the God of the Holy Bible, whose Word and Ways are simple, as is He (Romans 1:18). Justifying the wrath of God that comes down on the wicked, the author of the Book of Romans states clearly that no one can rightly claim ignorance of the Word, "since what may be known about God is plain to them, because God has made it plain to them. For since the creation of the world, God's invisible qualities— His eternal power and divine nature-have been clearly seen; being understood from what has been made, so that men are without excuse" (Romans 1:20).

The Word of God was designed to be understood by all, as in Romans 1:18. How, then, or why, then, do we allow the multitudes of charlatanic Christians to get away with their glitzy chicanery? Those who choose to feed on chaff become as weightless as chaff. Where do you stand?

What the Good Book says is as clear and readily available to us as the Power, Might, and Glory of the Lord that are exhibited in His creation each day and every season. We comprehend the written Word in much the same way that we comprehend our glorious surroundings: spiritually. The greatness of the artist Michelangelo is not in his words but in the virtuosity on display in his work, such as the paintings on the ceiling of the Sistine Chapel or his statue of David. We need not understand the history and nature of the Italian High Renaissance in order to grasp Michelangelo's inspired, transcendent creations. A picture or sculpture or symphony is worth a thousand words. Art is a universal language. In saying so, in no way do I denigrate the Word of God. Of course not! For I cherish and honor the Presence and Word of God more than anything. The point is that, as willing, believing readers of His Word, we intuit the True Meaning of the Words in a way that is similar to how we sense the essence of Michelangelo's David. We read the Holy Bible spiritually.

In my diatribe against God-forsaking, charlatanic Christian exhibitionists, I am not at all condemning God-commissioned, Christ-inspired efforts to explain Wondrous Mysteries of God to the people of the world. Certain divinely inspired commentaries are welcome because they really do help us understand what we have not yet understood. But I, alongside Connie, stand against all Christian marketeering and racketeering that insidiously demotes the Infallible Word of God, the Infinite, in order to bring power, goods, and money to church pretenders. We, the people, must make up our minds about what to believe: the Whole Word of God or the adulterated, bastardized version, which clearly represents unrepentance, agnosticism, or outright unbelief. Advocates of postmodernist humanism slither into pulpits and pews everywhere with one outcome in mind: bringing down the Church of Jesus Christ, Adonai's sanctuary. Our intention must be to fulfill John Milton's declaration in *il Penseroso*: "Bring all heavens before their eyes." May God's Will be done!

Replacement of the Bible

The "new bibles" and their literature compiled from mankind's imaginings replace the Whole Word of God spoken by God to chosen men and women. The congregation is subtly coerced into abandoning the Word for the worldly ideas of church "leaders" infatuated with power and money. They are megalomaniacs with appetites for materialism that rival those of Hollywood actors. They aspire to fraternize with the rich and famous members of the exclusive cult of humanism and modernism. The only difference is that they meet in church buildings, temples, and synagogues.

Friends, our bottom line is that we need not read, listen to, or look at everything written, or recorded, or broadcast, or drawn by so-called men and women of God. We need not fear them either, for the Holy Bible counsels that the fear of the Lord is the beginning and sustainer of wisdom but the fear of man brings a snare. Adonai has given us, not a spirit of fear, but a spirit of power and soundness of mind.

Adonai and His Word are immutable. Anyone who challenges either, whether pastors, bishops, popes, or laity, should be renounced. Atheism, agnosticism, and deism all have a new face. Let us be careful and hearken to God's Wisdom spoken through Solomon in Ecclesiastes12:12: "Be warned my son of anything in addition to them [see also Ezra 9:8]. Of making many books there is no end, and much studies wearies the body." Here is the conclusion of the matter: "Fear God and keep His Commandments, for this is the whole duty of man" (Ecclesiastes 12:13).

APPENDIX SEVEN

Seminary Education, Intellectual Sophistication, and the Making of the Unholy Bible

A diploma in theology is a good thing since it generally facilitates better understanding of theology. However, it is imperative that we differentiate between theology as the study of deities and religions, and theology as the study of the Holy Scriptures, leading to knowledge of and intimacy with the Godhead. Also, seminary education should never be the only qualification for mounting the pulpit to address a gathering of God seekers. It is indeed unfortunate that a seminary diploma is fast becoming the prime prerequisite for recognition in religious circles, appointment to positions of spiritual leadership, and possession of a "certificate to evangelize." Many believe, and wrongly so, that to have a true comprehension of the Word and the Will of God, one needs a seminary education. What a stumbling block! It matters not in what room one studies—seminary classroom, boardroom, bedroom, kitchen. If Professor Holy Ghost is not present, the student's time is wasted, Truth is compromised, and adulterated versions of the Word of God are disseminated. So goes the "value" of contemporary seminary education to 21st-century Christianity!

Given such proliferation of wrong teachings by self-ordained oracles of God, let us end with an anointed prayer by a truly anointed servant of God: Leonard Ravenhill, a true mentor:

MY PRAYER FOR PREACHERS
by Leonard Ravenhill

Eternal Father,
In the majesty of Thy glory,
Look down in mercy on these men.

As they enter their seclusion as preacher,
May they emerge from it as prophets.

According to Your promise, give them a new heart.
According to Your Holy Word,
Put a new spirit within them.
Anoint their eyes with holy eye salve
That they may see what heretofore they have not seen.

Unstop their ears that they may hear Your voice
In a way You could not previously speak to them.
Touch their lips with a live coal from the altar of eternity
that they may step back into time
like men who have tasted the powers of the world to come.
Grant that their theology
May become almost a theophany.

In these days of Noah-like society,
When the earth again is corrupt before Thee
And when violence has become a way of life,
And sexual immorality a sport;
When iniquity is legislated

And unborn babes are mutilated in the womb;
In this dread hour, challenging Thee to judge us,
Grant these men compassion
And a passion, motivated by the love of Thy Son,
For doomed humanity.

We tremble as we see
The over-blest, over-fed, over-come nations
Wallow in sin
On the brink of destruction;
As we see that
The law of the day is lawlessness,
The faith of the day is faithlessness,
The philosophy of the day is hopelessness,
The evident condition of the Church is powerlessness.

In this unprecedented state of moral anarchy
And spiritual debility,
Let these men not dare to see the faces of men again
Until they are renewed in the Holy Ghost.

If these men are not the men to shake the nation
Before the King comes,
Then in mercy find such men to shake earth and hell,
And fill heaven with praise
That He has seen of the travail of His soul
To His satisfaction.

Emeka Anonyuo, Ph.D.

These things I ask
In the name of and for the glory of
The only Savior of men,
Jesus Christ our Lord,
Amen.